THIS BO— —LONGS TO

HIGHLAND DEER FOREST

By the same author:

HIGHLAND YEAR

HIGHLAND
DEER
FOREST

L. MacNally

ILLUSTRATED WITH 76 PHOTOGRAPHS
BY THE AUTHOR

J. M. DENT & SONS LTD
LONDON

For my mother and father, and for
the Highland stalker, a race of men
dwindling, alas, who have been truly
called 'the salt of the earth'.

First published in 1970
© Text and illustrations, L. MacNally, 1970
© *The 'Barren' Hill*, Hugh MacNally, 1970

Made in Great Britain
at the
Aldine Press · Letchworth · Herts
for
J. M. DENT & SONS LTD
Aldine House · Bedford Street · London

ISBN 0 460 03955 5

Contents

Illustrations

Foreword

By THE time this book is in print I shall have gone from Culachy, that place wherein I spent nineteen happy and fruitful years, so much so that I would have been content to spend my life in it. It was not to be however, but neither my family nor I can ever remember Culachy without nostalgia.

Culachy is a Highland estate, in the heart of the Great Glen, in Inverness-shire, stretching ten miles north and south, from Loch Ness to the summit of Corrieyairack. Through it, indeed bisecting it, runs the right-of-way of General Wade's military road, engineered between the 1715 and 1745 rebellions as an aid in keeping the 'savage' Highlanders in check. From it, on most days of the year, red deer may be seen, 'by those with eyes to see', and the expectation is ever-present of seeing a golden eagle glide high over hill and glen.

A 'kindlier' estate in terrain than many, its lower reaches are luxuriant in birches, interspersed with rowan, hazel and bird cherry, its centre typical West Highland heather and deer-grass-clad moor-land and hill, and its higher ground swelling up to green, stone-scattered ridges of the type beloved by ptarmigan.

Such variety of terrain ensured a similar variety, indeed richness, of wild life, both winged and four-legged, from those of wooded glen to those of high tops. It is of encounters with this rewarding variety of wild life that I write in the ensuing pages in the hope that those reading of them will have as much enjoyment as I had in experiencing them.

It is saddening to reflect, however, that Culachy is also symbolic of the gradual decline which is overtaking Highland estates nowadays, a decay accelerated since the Second World War. The hill-paths, superbly engineered in the late 1800s, in the heyday of grouse and deer, have progressively accelerated in decay with the collapsing of the key-bridges along their ways. At one time a man had been employed *full-time* in maintaining these: later, workers from the farm had done sufficient to keep them usable: later still the 'private staff' at the lodge, of chauffeur, gardener and stalker, had done this. With progressive cutting down of both farm workers and private staff this maintenance had become impossible eventually, as happened on so many Highland estates, where understaffing became a 'Highland evil'. While the official cry was still, 'Avert depopulation in the Highlands' little was done to aid *estates* to do this by maintaining families in traditional Highland employments. Increased mechanization, higher wages and taxes and finally the iniquitous burden of Selective Employment Tax ensured that more and more natives left the glens and the employments they had been used to. When I went to Culachy first the private staff consisted of a housekeeper, cook, chauffeur, gardener and stalker. On the farm were a manager whose wife was employed in the dairy, a cattleman with a son and daughter also employed, two shepherds with an extra helper at lambing-time, and three farmhands, a maximum of sixteen. When I left there were a farm manager whose wife helped in the dairy, one shepherd, two farmhands and myself, a stalker.

Of the proprietors who owned Culachy during my nineteen years there I remember with particular affection Mr and Mrs Neil Usher. They were *resident* landowners who entered fully into, and enriched in every sense, the community life of the area. Culachy and Fort Augustus were the poorer for their going. I am, personally, deeply in their debt for their encouragement and help in my writing and photography, while they were in Culachy.

I must also record my gratitude to those others, mainly stalkers, who helped me in obtaining materials and photographs. They are too numerous to list but I would mention my brother Hugh (to whom I am also indebted for the use of his poem, 'The "Barren" Hill'); Major W. G. Gordon of Glenquoich; 'Jock' MacPherson, one-time stalker on Glendoe as his father and grandfather before him; Willie MacDonald, stalker on Aberchalder; Duncan Stoddart, stalker on Cluanie; and George Stoddart and Roddy MacRae, stalkers on Glenquoich. I am honoured to think of these men as my friends.

Finally, I would like to thank the editors of the *Scots Magazine*, the *Shooting Times* and *The Field* for permission to reproduce material used at some time in their pages.

I would conclude by drawing attention to the fact that there are many societies today which one can join and so help to safeguard our heritage of wild-life and its habitats in Britain. Those which I particularly know of are the British Deer Society; the Scottish Wild Life Trust; the Scottish Ornithological Club; the National Trust for Scotland; and the Royal Society for the Protection of Birds. All of these are worthy of support in an era when, without their vigilance, we might lose much which cannot be replaced.

THE 'BARREN' HILL

The noble stag and watchful hind gaze proudly from the hill,
Probing the peaceful scene below with eye that's never still.
The golden plover sounds again his plaintive eerie cry;
A wild cat stops to look—then hurries by.

The raven calls 'kruk! kruk!' from up in space
Above the scattered deer on sheltered face,
And viewing all below with cold assessing stare,
The golden eagle soars, *élite*, with silent grace.

The cock grouse, wary on his tussock stance,
A sentinel watching with an air of arrogance;
Scattered through the hags his busy brood,
Weaving and bobbing in their search for food.

Whilst high upon the ridges, ptarmigan croak,
Safe from the eye, their plumage being the perfect cloak;
And by the roots of long forgotten pine in hags below,
A mouse prepares his larder for the coming snow.

In heather deep the red fox curls to have his sleep,
Repleted by his midnight feast of carrion sheep;
And as the sun grows stronger in the sky,
He hears the sound of honking geese go by.

Then suddenly the grouse 'cock! cocks!' his warning cry;
The wary hind jumps up, her 'bark!' an urgent plea:
A man comes up the burn, by yonder tree.
The grouse lie low. The deer all turn and flee.

The raven wheels, 'kruk! kruks!' again in louder tone,
The eagle fades away to find a quieter zone;
The red fox slips into a nearby scree,
While danger stalks the hill for all to see.

For wildlife lives in balance, where nothing kills for joy,
With man the one offender to this old survival law.
Where Nature in her wisdom does every beast employ,
Man, so wise, yet ignorant, seeks only to destroy.

HUGH MACNALLY

1

The Birth of a Deer Forest

A PROUDLY antlered stag splashing through the shallows of a swift-flowing burn, winding its way through a Highland strath. Behind, running at full stretch and gaining perceptibly, a couple of high-legged deerhounds, lean and grizzled, superficially similar in conformation to greyhounds, but larger and heavier and with wiry, curling, blue-grey coats. Still farther behind, much farther behind in fact, the toiling figures of two men, striving to keep the chase in view. Such a sight, usual enough in the Highlands of bygone days, may never be seen again.

The first use of deerhounds in coursing and pulling down deer is lost in antiquity, the hounds of Celtic and Ossianic mythology being almost as well-known as their legendary masters. An Ossianic account tells of a great deer-coursing in Skye in which three thousand deerhounds were loosed, each killing two stags, while the peerless Bran, 'though a whelp then', distinguished himself by killing three. Not content with this Ossianic bag of six thousand and one stags the hounds then 'fell in with', and killed one hundred wild boar. Whilst granting a generous amount of poetic licence to this account it is nevertheless certain that in those far-off days, with a dearth of effective long-range weapons, the possession of a good deer-hound capable of keeping the larder stocked must have been of very great value.

The eventual introduction of firearms and their steady improvement in range and accuracy spelled the inevitable end of the use of

3

deerhounds as a means of obtaining meat, though, mainly as a legacy
of a traditional Highland sport, they were still in vogue in the mid-
1800s. According to Charles St John in his well-known works on the
Highland sport and wild life of that era, coursing was less satisfying
than stalking deer with a rifle, and this, mark you, was still in the era
of the black powder muzzle-loaders. St John's main objection was
that so often the whole run took place out of view, after the initial
laying on of the hounds, until the stag was perhaps found at bay in
some rocky burn. As much of the Highlands is rugged and broken in
terrain this would appear, so far as spectacle is concerned, to be a
valid objection. To lessen this disadvantage, in coursing for sport, the
hounds wherever possible were slipped only on favourable ground,
that is, a wide expanse of fairly flat and preferably softish ground
overlooked by commanding ridges. Deerhounds ran by sight and not
by scent and the deer, once spied from afar by the handlers, had to be
stalked with as much care as we use nowadays with the rifle, and with
the added difficulty of keeping a couple of eager hounds out of view
until within favourable loosing distance. Having got so far, a task
requiring great skill in approach work, the hounds were shown the
deer and at once slipped.

Invariably the fattest and heaviest stag in the group approached
would begin to lag behind and would be singled out for pursuit, and
on favourable ground, as above, the fleet hounds would gain on him.
Being hard-pressed the stag would take the easier downhill course,
and so inevitably, to a burn where, assuming he was not pulled down
en route, he might ultimately come to bay.

It was undoubtedly easier for the hounds to pull down a stag
while stretched in full run than by a frontal attack when the stag
came to bay. A good hound would overtake and range alongside its
quarry, balance itself, and while at full gallop leap for a throathold.
The force of the impact, delivered while pursued and pursuer were at
full stretch, threw the quarry and usually resulted in instantaneous
death with a broken neck. If, however, the deer came to bay backed
protectively into rocky wall or steep bank, the hounds had little
chance of pulling him down and if incautious, in a frontal attack,
might well fall victim to the lightning sweeps of the antlered head.
In many cases, if the stag gained the rough and sharp-stoned going
of one of the rocky, precipitous burns common in the Highlands,
he got clean away, being more sure-footed and faster in these
conditions than his pursuers.

4

This traditional Highland way of coursing was, on the whole, a reasonably even encounter between hounds and a stag who could, and often did, escape, over terrain with which he was completely familiar and who was capable at times of killing or disabling the hounds.

The last estate in the Highlands to use deerhounds extensively for coursing was that of Culachy, in Inverness-shire. Formerly land of the clan Fraser, Culachy was bought in the 1880s by a Mr M. K. Angelo, who shortly after his purchase began to breed hounds specifically for coursing. A man of very definite views, he tried to improve on the pure Scottish deerhound by cross-breeding with Irish wolf-hound, boarhound and borzoi. The borzoi was 'to give them drive'. They stood about thirty-four inches at the shoulder and weighed up to one hundred and thirty-five pounds in running condition. I have since been told that in gaining weight he probably lost in speed which was probably why most of the coursing with these hounds ended in a stag at bay, with as many as half a dozen of these huge hounds combining to pull it down. The pure-bred Scottish deerhound is a gentle dog, entirely dependable in nature, so much so as to appear incongruously fitted as a hound of the chase. The cross-bred hounds in use on Culachy were of a much more uncertain nature, however, and on at least three occasions in the memory of an old friend of mine, John MacDonald, (better known as Johnny Kytra after the old Highland custom of giving a man's Christian name the qualification of the place he lived at instead of a surname which might be legion in the area) they savaged intruders who had unwisely or unwittingly strayed into their high-fenced kennel yard. One intruder lingered thereafter in John's memory as, with an arm literally broken, and badly ripped, he kept exclaiming incoherently, when rescued, 'Lord Almighty, I've been all through the Boer war and never got wounded like this.'

The coursing at Culachy according to John, who as a youth worked as a dog handler on Culachy, was nearly always practised on an extensive boggy flat with hard ridges on its north and south, and a deer fence sealing off its west side. A winding, shallow burn, green-banked, wound its way across this flat, deepening abruptly, with rocky sides enclosing it, shortly before falling into the steep gorge of the river Tarff on its east side. To the harder 'going' of its banks, the pursued stag almost inevitably turned when pressed hard by the hounds, which were always taken in from the west side. The procedure was initially similar to traditional Highland coursing in that a couple of hounds were taken as close as possible to deer spied by their handlers and then loosed. While, however, this was going on another two couples of hounds were being positioned at intervals, out of sight in the burn down which the stag invariably was forced to turn. As a further precaution to prevent the escape of the stag, at a point in the burn near a shepherd's bothy, below which the banks steepened into the rocky gorge in which the stag might escape, an attendant was posted to turn or check the stag if he got so far.

These precautions rob the Culachy's coursing of much of its attraction for me, substituting a contest with scales heavily weighted against the stag for the traditional Highland mode of the duel between the pursued and one couple of hounds only. Nevertheless, there was much thrilling spectacle in this coursing. In the words of my old friend, a mine of information on Culachy from its early days as a deer forest, 'It was tremendously exciting to see the stag appear over a ridge, making straight as an arrow for us, as we hid in the burn ahead of him, with behind him, the first two hounds'. As soon as the chase came close the second couple was loosed. 'It was a sight to see, the stag jumping high in the air to clear the approaching fresh couple, the original couple hard behind, but, significantly he said, 'he did not jump high for long'. The third couple might be loosed if the stag proved strong enough to evade the first two, and occasionally, very occasionally, a stag would get as far as the watcher near the shepherd's house to be, as a rule, checked, to an inevitable fate.

Once, upon a warm day, on which the initial approach had been long and time-consuming, the shepherd-watcher, Murdoch by name, fell asleep, comfy in the heather, and a particularly strong and fleet-footed stag passed while he dozed. In due course the 'hunt', non-plussed at losing the stag, arrived at the now wakeful 'watcher'. 'Did you see the stag pass here, Murdoch?' inquired Angelo himself. 'No,' was the truthful reply. The disconsolate retinue continued down the burn and the shepherd's wife being at her door she was courteously asked if *she* had seen the stag. 'Yes,' said she, unaware of her husband's slumbering, 'it passed down the burn a wee while ago.' The trenchant, but only momentary silence, was broken by the anything but courteous Gaelic imprecation heaped on his spouse's head by Murdoch, too late to do anything but relieve his anguished feelings in thus being unwittingly betrayed by the wife of his bosom.

The Culachy hounds were occasionally injured but I have no record of any fatalities, though it was recalled by Johnny that one

6

hound was once carried home on an improvised stretcher, with a torn abdomen roughly stitched on the spot. It recovered to course again. This coursing, which apparently began around 1893, ended in 1912 with the death of M. K. Angelo, and though a few hounds were retained until 1915, wartime exigencies in maintaining a kennel of these large hounds ultimately led to the end of them, and to the end, by and large, of deer-coursing in the Highlands.

It is hard for any one of us contemporary with a particular era to visualize the scene so different from that of our own day, and I shall always be grateful to Johnny Kytra for his memories of Culachy, affording as they do insight into the great changes which occur even in areas like the Highlands, which have probably lingered 'in the past' more than any part of Britain.

To me, it is well nigh inconceivable to think of Culachy without red deer, but so it apparently was, or at least relatively so, in the years prior to about 1890. The high ground of Culachy held in those years a large stock of sheep, a wether stock maintained for their mutton, looked after by Johnny Kytra's father. He and his family lived in a small stone house well out on the hill, their link with the village of Fort Augustus being the old military road, engineered by General Wade to facilitate the movements of troops, between the 1715 and 1745 rebellions. Up this rough road a farm-cart took the bulkier provisions but, said Johnny, 'my mother would have to walk, sometimes with a baby in her arms for any small necessity she was out of'. It was a hard, spartan existence, with oatmeal, potatoes and milk the staple diet, and the main meat 'braxy' mutton, this being the meat of any sheep which happened to die, a perquisite of shepherds in those days and a diet on which their families were reared. 'I have seen my father return from church on a Sunday, and, *without putting off his Sunday clothes*, enlist the aid of one of us children to go and "bleed" and collect a dead sheep which he had been informed by a drover had died that morning as they approached Fort Augustus with a huge drove of sheep.' The rush was in case somebody else found the sheep first, a great windfall in those frugal days. This was in later years after the family had moved to Kytra, much nearer to Fort Augustus on the edge of the Caledonian Canal. Johnny's mother, though glad to be nearer the village, forever cherished memories of her lonely house in the hills. 'I can see the sky above it,' she was wont to say wistfully at times, gazing over the ridges of hills which hid all else from her. The woman's role was hard indeed, as wife of a hill shepherd. To her fell

7

all the household chores and much of the work in caring for the cow and pig which were necessities then, besides rearing a large family. The man was the wage provider, his daily paid work was an almost sacred obligation, and when this was done it was his leisure time. To help in the house was unthinkable.

The sheep which Johnny's father looked after on Culachy were those of the farming tenant. Shooting, of grouse and hares (prior to the 1880s) was leased by a shooting tenant in the season, and this tenant brought his own keeper with him, the ground being otherwise keeperless. The shepherds were expected to keep down hooded crows and, *in winter*, to reduce the numbers of the swarming blue hares. They also helped the 'fox-hunter', a man in those days who went from estate to estate over a wide area, using a motley 'pack' of terriers with a nondescript hound or two, to keep down the foxes. A muzzle-loader of dubious looks but unquestionable killing powers formed his armament.

For keeping down the hares *in winter*, the shepherd was supplied with a small amount of powder and shot for use in a muzzle-loader, also supplied by the farming tenant, but this ammunition often ran out with many hares yet to kill. He then used his collies, which he had trained to 'point' at a tussock which concealed a close-lying hare while he crept up with a stick through which was a large nail forming a spike in its head. With this improvised 'knobkerry' he killed many hares each winter, for in those days 'there would be a hare beside every stone'. Grouse, too, were numerous, three hundred brace in a season being normal, without driving or any management outwith the shooting season.

It must have been a matter of irony to the shepherd that the hares, vermin to the farming tenant because they ate the grazing he thought better utilized in feeding his sheep, were game to the shooting tenant in August, though I am assured that on grouse days orders were often given *not* to shoot many hares as they were so heavy to carry.

This conflicting viewpoint caused Johnny's father financial loss and no doubt some heart-searching in one year. He was out working at peats (the staple fuel for the family) with his wife on an August morning in the grouse season, and his collies caught two young hares. Going home for lunch the hares were hung from the rafters of the single room to form in due course a welcome item on the menu. When husband and wife returned to their work at the peats the door was, as always, left unlocked. Later that day the shooting tenant passed, after a good day at grouse, and told his southcountry keeper to leave a brace of grouse with the shepherd, in recognition of his attacks at the hoodies. One look inside and the keeper returned to his master, still carrying the brace of grouse. 'You've little need to leave grouse there,' he said, 'the house is like a game larder.' On reaching home the shooting tenant complained bitterly to the shepherd's employer. No explanations were asked for, the shepherd got no grouse and his annual length of tweed with which to have a suit made was denied to him that year, a serious loss, even though a colleague assured him that he had lost little 'as it was hardly worth having made-up'.

This was before M. K. Angelo acquired Culachy, in the era when deer forests were just beginning to come into vogue, and to supplant sheep, at that time more numerous than deer in many parts of the Highlands, but sheep-farmers were now in financial difficulties after their century of reign in the Highlands following the notorious and well-documented cruelties of the 'Clearances' in the late 1700s.

About 1890 the shepherd was moved to the house at Kytra. Under the ownership of Angelo, the sheep were to be cleared off the forest so as to encourage red deer from an adjacent established deer forest to the east of Culachy to colonize the ground now left quiet. This they did, so successfully and rapidly that in five years' time some sheep were re-introduced, and since then deer and sheep have co-existed on Culachy. A high deer fence was erected right around the west and south boundaries so as to keep the 'acquired' deer from, in turn, colonizing 'sheep-ground' to south and west of Culachy. An attempt was made to get the neighbouring estates to share in the march fence as a *deer* fence but this they would not agree to; in fact, they would not agree to the common march fence *being* a deer fence. The situation then arose whereby Angelo, determined to have his deer stopped from straying, erected a deer fence which, however, he was forced to keep sixteen yards *inside* the march or boundary, leaving the actual march fence as the normal sheep or stock fence. The lines of these two fences are there to this day, both in decay now, as evidence of the amount of money which could be spent in the Highlands on estate management in those days, and of the lack of liaison between estates. The deer fence, at least on the high ground, proved a complete failure. In its first winter snow, severe frosts and the fierce winter gales of the exposed top broke the wires and bent and twisted many of the stout iron standards. Nowadays, deer move

9

freely through it, from south and west as well as east, as wind and weather dictates, for, shortly after Culachy encouraged deer, the former sheep estates to south and west began to establish themselves as deer forests, this being thought to be more rewarding than the 'out of favour' sheep at that particular time.

There was, for a time, a thriving market in bottle-reared deer calves from recognized deer ground, where they were searched for on the hill at calving time, reared on cow's milk in large pens, and eventually transferred to grounds aspiring to form deer forests. Stocks were augmented by colonization on land adjacent to deer ground, the deer 'migrants' encouraged by the burning of heather which in due course created attractive new grazing, and by the removal of sheep stocks and a 'no shooting' policy for some years. Stags were also introduced from parks in England in many cases, in attempts to form good breeding stock. On Culachy I have heard of only one such introduction. About the end of the Boer war a big stag arrived, from the Duke of Bedford, I am told. He arrived bereft of antlers, these having been sawn off for ease in transport. For some weeks he was kept in a large cattle shed until it was judged time, in late April, to get him to the hill. The question was how to get hold of the animal, in the large shed, and into the cart which was to take him to the hill. An estate-hand who was inclined to be a 'know-all' and therefore unpopular at times, volunteered to do the job, and advanced into the spacious shed armed with a large grain sack which he intended to drape over the stag's head and so blindfold him. The stag, of course, was just beginning to grow his new antlers at that time of year.

The intrepid would-be 'catcher' advanced, and the stag retreated, backing and backing until he could back no more, when with one lightning action he reared up on his hind-legs and smote the man to the ground with a flailing foreleg. It seems he was stunned for old Johnny told me, with a wicked grin, 'he was trailed out by the legs and dumped in the burn to come round'. The stag was eventually roped and afterwards released on the hill, with an identifying collar around his neck. He was seen only once thereafter, no further trace dead or alive ever being found of him.

And so from mainly sheep, and few deer, many hares and, relatively, many grouse in the 1880s, Culachy has come to, in the 1960s, a 'mixed' economy of sheep *and* deer, with hares so scarce as to be worthy of remark and grouse stocks also at a low level. Have the

10

larger stronger grazers and utilizers of heather and hill helped to supplant the smaller, the hares and grouse? Or is it that the West Highlands are wetter and with less good heather than a hundred years ago? Whatever the reason, in this area hares have gone and grouse are relatively few. We are lucky in having so many other forms of wild life in the area to maintain constant interest, if not economic return, and of these I will write in the ensuing chapters.

2

Experiences with Eagles

WHILE deer, mountain hare and grouse have waxed or waned very considerably in numbers here over the past century the status of the golden eagle has not altered appreciably. There is still a pair always in residence in a long and narrow glen, remote from human habitation and seldom visited except by shepherd or deer-stalker.

Eagles a century ago, and indeed until relatively recently, were not regarded favourably by shepherds, who alleged they habitually killed lambs, or by keepers, who knew that they killed grouse. As much of the Highlands then had sheep or grouse, or both, it can be seen that the overall climate of opinion of the men on the spot was distinctly anti-eagle.

Johnny Kytra's first memory of eagles is of his father chasing and swiping at, with his stick, very much with malice aforethought, a gorged eagle which he had surprised at the carcase of a dead wether. So gorged was it that it had great difficulty in taking wing and he almost got it with his stick, before it at last gained a rise in the glen bottom in the form of a small hillock, which enabled it to become airborne.

He told me of annual rounds of the eagles' eyries, well known on traditional nesting sites for generations, timed if possible to coincide with that period towards the end of April when the female was sitting tight awaiting the imminent hatching of her eggs after a long incubation period of some forty-two days. The female might then, at

13

the very climax of her incubation period, be cold-bloodedly shot on the nest as she peered, momentarily immobile in her surprise, at men suddenly materializing near her eyrie: for it came as a matter of great surprise to me to find out just how many eyries *can* be approached unseen. More often, perhaps, she might be shot as she flopped awkwardly off the nest, in her initial clumsiness of flight before she got enough 'wing space' to demonstrate her superb mastery of the air, her element.

Despite almost a century of persecution, however, eagles maintained a constant pair in this glen and bred almost annually until, in 1962, a new threat, in the apparent effect of Dieldrin, as used in sheep dips, began to be noticeable. In their consumption of carrion, of dead sheep, which is a regular feature of eagle diet, eagles ingested this toxic insecticide, among others, and from 1962 until 1968 one pair I watched had no breeding success whatever. In other areas of the North West Highlands similarly affected, there are now (1969) signs that a revival in breeding success is under way now that a ban on the use of Dieldrin in sheep dips has been in force for a year or two. It may be that this will become apparent here also. It is ironic to reflect that, quite inadvertently, the use of modern highly toxic chemicals in controlling various insect pests could almost have achieved what a century of direct premeditated persecution failed to do.

I have always been keenly interested in eagles, since, as a boy, I listened eagerly to tales related to me by an old shepherd of the eyries in the glen already mentioned. 'There is a cartload of sticks in one of them,' he was fond of saying, and, having, in later years, visited this eyrie site, now disused, I can vouch for the probability of this apparently Baron Munchausen statement. It is under a cave-like overhang and, situated on a shelving slab of rock, must have required a massive building up of its outer edge.

Huge as it must have been, this eyrie and the others in the glen eluded my youthful searchings, probably because I was looking for eyries on large, sheer faces of rock, whereas I now know that a ridiculously small outcrop of rock can hold an eyrie. The one common factor in all the eyries I have seen is an overhang above the actual structure, while there is usually at least one smallish rowan tree adjacent, and often, incongruously, a patch of rose bay willowherb below an eyrie.

It was not until I returned home to Fort Augustus after the last war, with a renewed zest for things Highland, that I began to

14

accumulate knowledge about eagles in the neighbourhood, and by this I mean within a radius of about twenty miles from my home. Ultimately I gained knowledge of four pair of eagles in the glens around me. In a period of ten years or so I made over one hundred and fifty visits to eyries, involving a distance of over two thousand miles, mainly afoot, visits packed with interest.

There have been moments of delight, as when I first discovered a tenanted eyrie and lay above it, hearing a rending, cracking noise as the female, unaware of my presence, tore a grouse apart to feed the eaglet. Of surprise, as when I saw a large dead stoat, a tough, rank meal, indeed, lying on an eyrie beside the two eaglets, and wonderment when I saw for the first time an adult fox as prey. Of revulsion when first I saw the remains of a red deer calf below an eyrie: on July 2nd 1960 I noted: 'I found, lying below the eyrie cliff, the forelegs of a very young red deer calf. The little hoof was black and some grains of peat were apparent on its under surface so that the calf had been at least a couple of days old, definitely not a still-born one. The leg, minus the shoulder-blade, had been picked clean, down to the mid-leg joint.' This was also the first indication I had seen of the habit of the adult eagle in removing the larger, inedible bones of prey from the nest and carrying them, for some distance at times, before dumping them.

Of near-panic, when I was temporarily lost in mist, on ground strange to me, in the middle of a remote, high and featureless, peat-hag-ridden plateau. To make matters worse I had my ten-year-old son, Michael, with me that day. We had visited an eyrie on a day when mist was lowering and lifting intermittently and on our way back crossing this high ground plateau with which I was relatively unfamiliar, the mist insidiously crept lower around us until we could see no farther than a few yards. Twice, yes, three times, I found we were retracing our own footprints, discernible here and there in the soft peat, had wandered, in fact, completely off course, and at times were obviously going in circles in the innumerable, superficially similar, hollows and peat hags, dotted with lochans. All were maddeningly alike as their steel-grey waters lapped at their shores, dimly visible before they faded into obscurity in the mist which shrouded most of their surface. Eventually I managed to retrace my steps to above the glen which held the eyrie and we had a sandwich while I tried to compose my thoughts. While we did so, luckily, the mist lifted, only fleetingly but enough for me to strike a line to where

15

a distinct path led homewards. It is an extremely nasty and 'helpless' feeling, to be 'wandered' on unfamiliar and remote ground in thick mist, and one I would not care to repeat, certainly not with a ten-year-old dependent on one's 'infallibility'. Mist, in fact, was a constant hazard in visiting this particular glen, which involved climbing over a fairly high mountain massif before descending into the remote glen which held this pair of eagles. On 6th July 1963 I noted: 'The mist was even worse than on last Saturday, down in a smoky blanket to low ground level. Once I left the road I could not see six feet ahead. Managed fairly well, nevertheless, until I got half-way, then went off course and had to retrace my steps to find it again. Reaching, at last, the whereabouts of the eyrie I had a job finding it. On similar occasions before the eaglet had been "cheeping" on the eyrie and I had located it by ear, today it was silent, indeed the silence was almost eerily tangible as the grey mist swirled around me. When I did eventually come in sight of the dead tree directly below the eyrie, its bleached, fallen trunk looming through the mist, it was to see the female eagle perched on a bare, barkless branch. She sat breast-on to me, huge and yet indistinct even in her nearness, and only flew, straight over my head, when I was almost upon her. The thin branch whipped up and down for moments after her departure, the thrust of her weight leaving it imparting a liveliness to the dead wood.'

There were disappointment and anger, too, on the occasion when I found an eyrie deserted, the eggs cold, and heard later that the female had been shot. I had wondered if both male and female shared the incubating duties and at this eyrie I had definite proof that they do, for on returning a few days later to be absolutely sure that the eggs were deserted I found the cock incubating. I wondered if he would confound the slayers of his mate in hatching the eggs but, of course, he did not persevere and the eggs never were hatched. Even if he had hatched them he would not have been able to cope in rearing the young, which for the first few days would have needed almost continual brooding, the female's role, leaving the male no time to fulfil his own role of hunting for food. The male eagle has no instinct to tear up prey and feed the young, and in eagles this is necessary for five to six weeks after hatching. Again, this is the female's role, a role common to the females with our other birds of prey also, and I have heard of eaglets (and young buzzards) dying, surrounded by maggot-infested prey, brought in faithfully by the male after his mate's death,

16

Johnny Macdonald (Johnny Kytra), stalker on Culachy for forty years, who had a fascinating fund of anecdotes of Culachy in days gone by.

I

II

A present-day pure-bred Scottish deerhound, high of leg and wiry of coat, a dog of kindly nature despite its impressive size.

When a herd of stags was coursed by the deerhounds the fattest and heaviest would fall behind and might fall victim to the deerhounds.

IV

Michael, my companion on many an eagle expedition, holding a three-week old eaglet.

On my visit in early May one egg was hatching and I could see, and hear, the eaglet within. A week later both eggs had hatched, the tiny eaglets dwarfed by the huge parent eagle.

Eaglets of six weeks old at the eyrie which was watched weekly until the survivor of the two eaglets left it, at ten weeks old.

An eaglet, at eight weeks old impressive in size and strength but not yet ready to leave the eyrie. It was the survivor of two eggs hatched.

VII

A nine-week old eaglet, hunched protectively over the prey taken in by one of the parents, in this case the remains of a red deer calf.

Two handsome eaglets, near to flying stage. In a year when prey is scarce only one eaglet may survive from the two hatched.

diligently hunting but blindly uncomprehending of the need of the young to be fed piecemeal on the prey.

Regarding the sharing of incubation duties, in a later year I was fortunate in witnessing a 'change-over' at an eyrie. From my notes on 4th May 1963: 'Witnessed a change-over today as I sat resting while still some way from the eyrie. I was out of sight of the eyrie's occupant and some 800 yards away from, and below it. As I watched I saw an eagle rise up on the eyrie, to fling off it and fly east along the glen. Almost at once, as if at a signal, another eagle flew into view from *behind* the high ridge above the glen and glided across to join the first. I got the impression then that this second eagle was the larger, seeing them together in the air. The two soon separated, and the second eagle flew directly but unhurriedly along the face and alighted on the eyrie: disappearing as it began to incubate.'

Moments of instinctive fear there have been too, when I was 'buzzed' in determined low-level attacks by an irate female eagle. An animate projectile approaching one's head at incredible speed, with a wing-span of over seven feet and a body weight of eleven pounds with formidable steel hooks of talons lowered and spread as on business bent is quite intimidating. Luckily, this is very definitely rare with eagles, only two females, in widely separate glens, in 1959 and in 1963, have ever treated me thus. Of the 1959 one I have written in *Highland Year*, but the 1963 bird was even more determined and came much closer in her intimidating attacks. On 13th July 1963 I visited the eyrie in question to find the eaglet, at exactly ten weeks old, gone. From this eyrie it could have walked out onto the hillside and so I searched around on the supposition that at ten weeks it could not yet have reached expert flying stage. And then 'Ma' arrived, the nerve-racking 'Swoosh' from behind—which, each time, no matter how often repeated, caused the blood involuntarily to drain from my face—being, as usual, my first warning. I hurried forward to the dubious shelter of a small rock outcrop and bending down, took off my bag with its cameras inside, the eagle patrolling above as I did so. Immediately I stood up, head just above the outcrop, she banked and came straight at me. I now had my camera out, loaded with colour film, and tried to photograph her as she came at me, but no sooner was she apparent in the distance in the viewfinder than she seemed to be filling it, causing me to duck and to try to 'click' the shutter at the same time. She at once came round again and at me, starting her shallow swoop when about four hundred

17

yards away. A most impressive sight she presented, her golden head low between her shoulders, beak and eyes seemingly lined out on my eyes, legs and talons dropped and spread at about an angle of 60°, her wings held stiffly, half closed. She reminded me as she started her long, shallow but incredibly fast swoop, of a German Stuka dive bomber of the last war, peeling off for an attack, at first small, growing awesomely to intimidating size, before pulling out above and dwindling rapidly in the distance in prelude to another banking turn and another low-level attack. The eagle showed unmistakable animus that day, repeating her attack at least a dozen times, and though I tried to photograph her, using a speed of 1/250 of a second, all my photographs show movement. In extenuation of this I would offer the excuse that the photographs were taken under some slight difficulties.

The persistent aggression of the eagle was immediately understandable when, on her attacks ceasing, I found the eaglet was sitting on the hillside only yards above me. The female, in other words, was simply demonstrating strong maternal instinct in protecting her young one, now vulnerable in its relative inability to fly, and away from the comparative safety of the eyrie. Fox or wild-cat would have been similarly treated and would certainly then have put all thought of a meal of eaglet from their minds. As a rather stubborn even if temporarily intimidated photographer, I was in a rather different category, and I photographed and also caught and weighed the young eagle before leaving. It weighed nine and three quarter pounds at ten weeks old and was probably a female.

On visits to and from eyries the hill burns were a potential hazard whenever the weekends were wet, as they often were, for in attempting to form a chronological record, in notes or photographs, in the limited free time of weekends, one had to take the weather as it came.

The most unpleasantly hazardous day I had was because of heavy rain and fast-rising burns, and again I had Michael with me, in the same season as we were lost in the mist. From my notes, 8th May 1965: 'An absolutely shocking day, worst I've ever gone over to Glen B—— on,—and I had Michael with me. I had promised to take him, and the weather wasn't too bad when we left home. We had an hour's cycle run and then took to the hill. It had rained heavily all the previous night and I was a bit anxious about the height of the burns. We got across the first burn easily enough, dry-shod in fact, and started up the steep path. Rain was falling steadily now but we kept

18

hoping it would clear. As we gradually ascended higher a gale force wind met us and nearly halted us in our tracks more than once. Some thirty deer in the banks were very reluctant to go out of the relative shelter. In view of the weather we were to experience I can't blame them.

'By the time we reached the top of Glen B—— we were soaked through, but at least the wind had been at our backs in crossing the high ground plateau. No chance of spying at the eyrie in the wildness of the weather and, anyway, we were too wet to sit down. Below us, a string of deer ran past only fifty yards away, with us in full view, running up into the gale force wind and rain. To my mind came the words of an old stalker, 'In wild weather they [the deer] will jump over your head.' The biggish burn in the bottom of the glen made itself heard before we came to it and was already unpleasantly high. I had to carry Michael pick-a-back over, getting my knee-length rubber boots full of water as I did so. There was no point in even trying to empty them out, I would never have got them on again, and we had to return across the burn anyway. The last short, but very steep climb to the eyrie was sheer punishment, wicked, cold, grey spearpoints of rain slanting endlessly out of the west at us, dissipating further our flagging energies. One momentary rewarding thrill we got for as we came abreast of the eyrie the female, sitting facing the weather, cocked her head and looked full at us for all of half a minute before taking wing, to be carried out of sight by the gale in a flourish of widespread primaries. The eaglet was asleep and, as prey, a grouse lay near it. I took a photo and we left quickly: this was no day for lingering.

'Michael was almost at the limit of his endurance, cold, wet and tired, but still indomitable. When I blamed myself for taking him he said 'I *wanted* to come'. We paused for a moment near the glen bottom in the shelter of 'the Big Stone' at which, legend says, a woman and her babe died in the persecutions by the 'Butcher Cumberland', following the Battle of Culloden in 1746. After eating a bit of chocolate we very reluctantly left the Stone's relative 'warmth'; the burn below was still steadily rising in a smother of yellow-grey waters. With Michael on my back again I got fairly easily over the first bit but nearing the farther bank I was over my thighs in a deep, racing channel. I had to lean forward and slide Michael off over my head before I could pull myself out. We went up the steep face to the top as fast as our tired legs, weighted down by our clinging, saturated clothing, would allow and I now had Michael by the hand, too tired to demur. The top at last and a halt in the half-shelter of a hag to eat a sodden sandwich. I was dreading, for the ten-year-old boy's sake, the journey across the terribly rough terrain of that top plateau, *into* the teeth of the howling gale of wind and rain, chilling and strength sapping, but we had to get moving. Too long a rest meant getting too cold and chilled and too hard a pace, in an effort to keep warm, might exhaust Michael. I wondered if he could last out; would I have to carry him? I hadn't, though almost at the end of the roughest bit, he had to ask for a rest, near to tears, all honour to him. I sheltered him as best I could for five minutes then off again. The heavy rain was almost mist-like in its intensity now and I nearly went astray at one point. I do not exaggerate when I say it might have been the difference between life and death if we had, the conditions were shocking and we were utterly chilled, with soaked clothing.

'At last we got to the downhill stretch, warming up a little as we dropped lower out of that dreadful rain-laden wind. Everywhere, cataracts were spouting and bubbling out of the hillside and swirling fast over our path, eager to get to the burn below which we had yet to cross. We had crossed it dry-shod on our way out, how many punishing hours ago, but it was now raging, not a stone to be seen. I did not relish it one bit but cross we had to. With Michael up on my back again, I picked the widest part of the burn and stepped in. One cautious, probing step at a time, foot braced into the uneven, hidden bed of the torrent before I dared try another step, walking stick jammed into the burn bed downstream, helping to hold me against the current. The water was up to my waist and filled Michael's boots as he rode on my back. At one point I almost lost balance, but recovered; not a cheep from Michael at that horrible moment.

'We won over at last and reached our bikes a few minutes later. An excruciatingly cold business it was climbing into the saddles but a glorious relief to see the tarred road and find that Michael was able to ride his bike. Home at 5.30 p.m., after the worst and most worrying day I've ever had on the hill.'

A touch of comedy was afforded on one occasion when an almost fully fledged eaglet managed to grab my Weston exposure meter as I incautiously rested it on the edge of an eyrie, and retreated with this inedible prey to the farthermost corner of the eyrie. Luckily, I had the wrist cord of it firmly around my wrist and was able to pull it free from its new owner. The eaglet, balked of the indigestible meter, then grabbed a young grouse which lay on the eyrie, a distinctly audible 'scrunch' being heard as the talons went home. Retreating a little, it proceeded to eat it. The head was grasped first in the huge beak, the body being held down by both feet. A gentle twist and pull, almost as if the eaglet was gauging its resistance and then the head was pulled smoothly off and at once swallowed. The eaglet then pecked delicately at the protruding neck. Piece by piece was pulled off, sometimes only a piece of skin with feathers attached, all went down the capacious gullet. An entire wing came off, with a powerful wrench. The eaglet straightened up for greater ease in swallowing this but try and contort as it would, the wing wouldn't go down. At length the eaglet disgorged it and holding it down with one foot, pecked it to bits and swallowed it piecemeal. The breast was then tackled, bones and flesh, *all* went down, followed by the other wing, which was more expertly swallowed than the first, for it went down entire. A leg followed, vanishing easily, claws waving a macabre farewell as they disappeared. The internal organs followed, the entrails being rejected, however, though the leathery gizzard was pecked to bits and eaten. There remained one leg and this the eaglet, now obviously replete with bulging crop, picked up and swallowed almost absent-mindedly. It then made a positive lunge across the eyrie to my side and clapped its wings at me, raising a cloud of dust and feathers from the tawdry surface of the eyrie. And then, crowning indignity, it turned and began to elevate its stern in my direction. Knowing at once what was to follow and having a healthy respect for the force with which eaglet 'whitewash' was ejected, with visions of a white, sticky and messy camera and cameraman, I at once steered the eaglet broadside with my stick and as it let go with a liquid white jet, I photographed it.

Eagles, of course, are predators *par excellence* (though they eat more carrion than most people realize) and this is why they were, and are, unpopular in some quarters. To take the alleged killing of lambs first, in all my visits to eyries in over ten years, in an area devoted to sheep-farming, I have only seen lamb as prey on half a dozen occasions, and at times this was definitely carrion, as in the case of still-born lambs. As against this the wife of a friend of mine, living in one of the highest and most remote houses in Scotland, actually witnessed from the house an eagle lift and carry off a live lamb, and I was witness in another year to one or two definite lamb-kills on a

21

nearby estate. However, in my experience, of actual watching and noting prey over ten years, at many eyries lamb seldom features, and though an occasional pair of 'rogue' eagles will kill lambs this should not be taken as reason for condemning the species. It should always be remembered that in Highland sheep farming many lambs die in their first few weeks of life, and both eagles and fox capitalize on this mortality.

Grouse are undoubtedly staple prey in areas where blue hare and rabbit are absent, yet the eagle takes a wide range of prey including predators on grouse, such as fox, wild-cat, stoat and hoodie. I have noted as prey over the years, grouse, ptarmigan, ring-ousel, gull and raven, hare, rabbit, voles, fox, stoat and, occasionally, red deer calf. The last named only began to appear near the end of the nesting period, usually in late June. I have no doubt that the few deer calves which are born dead or die shortly after birth are readily lifted but I also know that red deer calves are killed on occasion. I have seen an eagle lingering suspiciously, to my mind, day after day in a coire where I knew deer calves were being born daily, around mid June, and I once skinned a recently dead calf on which there was no outward sign of violence except the unmistakable talon punctures each side of the withers and, where the other foot had gripped, each side of the head. Pitiful as this was, the eagle kills for food and no one kills more for food (and indeed at times for no reason) than man himself.

Patience is often the very essence of wild life photography and I had to wait many years before I obtained photos from a hide of the adult eagles at an eyrie. Of all the eyries I know there was only one even remotely suitable for hide work and here the hide had to be built on a narrow ledge only six feet from the nest. I built a heather and moss hide here, on a framework of netting, in a year when the eyrie was not in use. It was five years before it was tenanted again, and then on a morning in mid May I had one of my most unforgettable experiences at an eyrie. Michael put me into the renovated hide at the eyrie, which contained two downy eaglets of about a week old, one noticeably larger than the other. The female arrived on the nest edge almost immediately Michael had gone, but left again with a 'swoosh' of wing. A moment later and the now demonstrably flimsy structure of my improvised hide shook and quivered as the eagle landed on it, within inches of my cowering head. It shook even more violently, showering bits of heather and moss down on me as she flung off and landed with a flap of wings on the eyrie. I could hardly contain my excitement at seeing her within six feet of me, her clear, light brown eyes apparently capable of piercing through my flimsy disguise and her plumage much paler than that of the very young eaglets I had watched attain full plumage in their eyries. Her head, and particularly the nape of her neck, were light golden-brown in shade. She settled on the chicks and I did not attempt any photos for half an hour, seeing her periodically heaved up on the nest by the tiny chicks she was brooding. She left after I'd taken a snap or two and was away for half an hour. During this time the larger chick spent most of her absence in pecking, really unmercifully, the smaller one, often about the head but at other times on whichever part of its body was nearest. Little wonder the smaller one vanished a few days later. This type of conduct is well known where two eaglets are hatched in an eyrie. In many cases the weaker of the two succumbs, yet on three occasions in ten years on three different eyries I have seen two eaglets reared successfully, in apparent amity. A lot probably depends on whether one eaglet is markedly smaller than its nest mate, or whether prey is scarce, when the weaker will succumb.

On a later occasion at the eyrie I watched from the hide the female eagle feed the now five-week-old eaglet. Before the female arrived the eaglet had tried vainly to eat some of a grouse which I'd watched the male eagle bring in, pulling, usually, at its most unrewarding bit, to wit, its upturned foot. The eaglet was fed in typical raptor fashion, titbits being pulled off the grouse by the female and proffered to the eaglet, who picked them from the beak of the female, until its hitherto flat crop bulged like an orange. When the soft innards became exposed the eaglet leaned forward and helped itself, thus learning gradually against the day when it would tear up prey for itself. It took half the grouse to satiate it, and it then crept under the breast of the female to sleep off its feed. It flew in the third week of July, having given me some unforgettable moments.

An interesting and rather puzzling habit which the eagle and the common buzzard share is that of adorning the nest at sporadic intervals with fresh greenery. One theory is that it is done to conceal the increasing foulness of the nest's surface due to prey remnants over the lengthy fledgling time, ten to twelve weeks in the case of eagles. This may be so: if it is, some pairs, as with humans, are more 'house-proud' than others, for the habit is very marked in some and almost absent in others.

It makes a pleasant surprise to find the trampled and tawdry surface of an eyrie rejuvenated by the addition of fresh greenery. From my notes again: 'The eyrie was bare of prey, but looked as if an attempt had been made to lay a fresh green tablecloth over its brown and trampled surface, so profuse was the layer of *dry* moss, heather and crowberry. The green, dry moss (i.e. not sphagnum moss) appeared to have been stripped from rock or scree.'

Greenery which I have seen used over the years featured rowan as definite first favourite, and included birch, dwarf willow, juniper, heather, crowberry, cowberry, blaeberry, common rush, wood rush, grey lichen, dry green moss, sphagnum moss and once a big clod of earth and grass.

Eaglets usually left the eyrie around the third week of July, the earliest noted leaving on 8th July and the latest on 23rd July.

In one year (1963) I weighed the two eaglets on an eyrie weekly. I knew the age of the first hatched exactly, as I had been present when the egg was chipping, the eaglet inside cheeping lustily, its black beak visible through the ragged hole in the rough shell of the egg. Weights and plumage stages were as under:

Age		smaller bird	larger bird
1 week	White down	8 oz.	1 lb.
2 weeks	White down	1 lb.	about 2 lb.
3 weeks	White down	2 lb.	about 4 lb.
4 weeks	White down	$2\frac{1}{2}$ lb.	about $5\frac{1}{4}$ lb.
5 weeks	First dark feathers on wing edges and tail edges	4 lb.	7 lb.
6 weeks	Piebald appearance, half down, half feathers	5 lb.	8 lb. 6 oz.
7 weeks	Overall dark appearance but for large downy patch on breast	$4\frac{1}{2}$ lb.	8 lb. 7 oz.
8 weeks	Well-feathered, except for head and downy breast patch	Dead	9 lb.
9 weeks	Head feathered now, a tawny brown in colour	—	$9\frac{1}{2}$ lb.
10 weeks	Apparently fully fledged	—	$9\frac{3}{4}$ lb.

The smaller of the two died owing almost certainly to a scarcity of prey. It was not actively ill-treated by the larger one but when the eaglets were left to tear up the prey for themselves, at about six weeks old, it was undoubtedly unable to compete for a fair share and, following a week of scarcity when it actually *lost* half a pound (see table), it died. I have since reproached myself that I might have taken the weaker eaglet home to rear but I believed, at the time, that it had a good chance to survive.

attempt to kill the adult foxes, keen to return to the den which held their cubs. On another occasion, he, and another shepherd, a rather simple-minded character, were out all night helping the fox-hunter at a discovered den which held cubs. The vixen was out and the fox-hunter and Johnny's father, armed with muzzle-loaders, took up strategic positions around the den to await her return, leaving the other shepherd to keep watch at the actual den. The vixen somehow ran the gauntlet of the two posted guns and the first the fox-hunter saw of her was as she neared the den. He swore she actually sniffed at the boots of the, literally it seemed, unconscious watcher at the den who had dozed at that critical moment. Having thus established the presence of a human to her satisfaction, or dismay, she decamped but this time came nearer the fox-hunter and he had a long shot at her with his heavily charged muzzle-loader. The vixen, seemingly unscathed, turned and ran in the direction of Johnny's father who, in turn, ran across to get around the corner of a knoll which now concealed her flight from him. Man and fox met almost face to face as they rounded the knoll and Johnny's father said later, 'She sprang high in the air and dropped dead. It was as if she had died of fright at my sudden appearance.' When she was skinned, however, one slug from the fox-hunter's muzzle-loader was found to have penetrated her vitals, causing her death just as the shepherd had confronted her.

Whisky, much cheaper in those far-off days, was an invariable comfort at these long vigils at dens, and it seems reasonable to believe that it may have helped the vixen at times to evade what should have been the watchful eyes of the hunters. In one case, two stalkers and a ghillie were faced with an all-night vigil at a huge cairn, in a wild glen, about twelve miles from Fort Augustus. The senior stalker had a pound in his pocket and with this he dispatched the ghillie to the village for provisions, including the all-important whisky. The ghillie apparently thought little of his twenty-four mile walk and duly returned with the provender and a big earthenware jar of whisky. The night which started out cold and dreary apparently ended in a warm, alcoholic haze, so much so that the second stalker who had come from a neighbouring estate, arrived home in his stocking soles, having walked all the way over the rough hill thus, and without the least notion of where he had left his boots.

Dens were at times discovered by shepherds alone on their rounds on the hill. In such a case they sometimes had to return over many miles of hill to inform a keeper, and the situation was complicated because of the fact that a returning vixen, smelling the human taint left by the discoverer, would at once shift her cubs. To prevent this it was the practice to leave an article of clothing, as a jacket or coat, at a discovered den, relying on the vixen's fears and aversion to the alien article, smelling strongly of man, to keep her from entering and shifting her cubs. It did not always work for I have a record of a jacket being actually pulled away from the entrance to a sandhole den and the den being empty when the perspiring keepers arrived at it. One of Johnny's fox yarns, told with tongue distinctly in his cheek, was of a like occasion when a shepherd elected to leave his cap at a discovered den. Keepers and shepherd arrived back eventually to find the cap missing, but the cubs still in the den. Stations were taken up around the den, and in the gloaming the vixen was shot as she came trotting in, head held high retriever fashion, and in her jaws the cap of the shepherd, *containing a dozen grouse eggs.* View this yarn with justifiable suspicion as we may, I was nevertheless told, many years later, by a stalker whose word I would rely on, that he had once shot a dog fox early one morning which had been carrying in its mouth the stomach-bag of a sheep, and inside this odoriferous 'shopping-bag', the carcase of a mole.

There has long been a tradition that the hill fox was of a longer, leggier breed than the typical low ground or English fox, of yellow-grey colouration and without the normal black markings on the legs. Old traditions die hard, but personally I have never seen such a fox nor do I know anyone who has. Those I have handled in the last twenty years have been exactly as the English fox, red of coat and with the usual black markings, while their weights were certainly no heavier, being around 11–12 lb. in vixens, and 14–15 lb. in dog foxes. Another theory widely held that a bold white tag to a tail indicated a dog fox is quite definitely incorrect. A vixen may have a beautiful white tag to her brush while her mate has a blackish tip, or vice versa.

Foxes are credited with great cunning and they are certainly creatures of resource, of supreme fitness and of absolutely hair-trigger reactions, in which they appear more feline than canine. Strangely enough, they are not really difficult to trap and the old-time gin-trap (as I write this, possibly soon to be banned in Scotland) accounted for many foxes. With its iron jaws and the fact that it held but did not kill its victim it was not a nice weapon in fox warfare and I, for one, will not regret its passing. Foxes were said to gnaw off a foot to free themselves from gin traps but again I have never had

29

experience of that. I have seen them held by perhaps only a sinew in a trap, bone and flesh having been broken by the strong spring and toothed jaws of the gin, and yet they had not attempted to gnaw through this slender 'tie'.

One of the very few palatable yarns of foxes and traps was told to me by Johnny Kytra. A stalker he knew found a fox in one of his traps and, hitting it on the head with his stick, he threw it to one side while he painstakingly reset the trap, taking about ten minutes to do this. When he turned around he had no fox; the animal, only stunned, had decamped, leaving the discomfited stalker to reflect wryly and profanely on the 'cunning' of the fox.

Perhaps the most remarkable fox and trap yarn I heard was from a shepherd, an absolutely reliable informant. He was going around the hill when he discovered a fox cub, alive, in a gin trap, with around it the remains of at least a dozen lambs and with the dry peat trampled and padded to the radius of the trap's chain. He killed the cub and, on examining it, judged it to be 'rolling in fat', and yet he estimated that it must have been about a fortnight in the trap. The keeper of that ground had been ill for some days and had not been able to go round his traps. It was obvious that the vixen, or perhaps both dog and vixen, had been bringing food to the trapped cub all the while it had been caught—faithfulness which perhaps deserved a better end than the eventual death of the cub.

Devotion to their cubs or to their mates perhaps is easily understandable yet I had a rather less understandable instance of apparent devotion of one fox to another, in April some years ago. A shepherd whom I knew was driving along an unfrequented hill road when he saw, quite near the road, what he took to be an old vixen bending over a dead deer calf. He stopped and left the car to investigate. The vixen, which he now saw to be very bedraggled looking, ran a little way off, then turned to look at him before retreating again, but only to the edge of a nearby birch wood. There she stopped, in view among the leafless trees, inexplicable behaviour in a species which shuns man like the plague, and began to skirl. Wondering, the shepherd approached the supposed deer carcase and then found it was another fox, a slim young vixen with a badly broken foreleg, too weak to move. Nevertheless she held her ears back and exposed sharp white fangs in a hissing snarl as he came near and so he went for a colleague, who possessed a gun. As the two men returned, some fifteen minutes later, the old vixen was *still* lurking in the trees and

30

still, as they described it, 'howling'. The injured fox was relieved of further misery, and the injury was, on examination, thought to be consistent with that which could have been caused by a light-weight, high velocity rifle bullet slicing at an angle on the shoulder blade. But how does one explain the older vixen's behaviour? The most obvious explanation was that she was trying to succour the younger vixen, which could have been her cub of the previous year, to the extent of even trying to drag her along to some cover. We tend to think of foxes as 'single' animals, except when mated and rearing cubs, but do we *know* this? It is conceivable that a young vixen might team up with the mother for its first winter. In this case it was found on investigation that the young vixen had not mated, and it is possible that the other, an obviously old vixen, had not mated either. There is unquestionably a strong attachment to their cubs on the part of vixens and an unwillingness or inability to recognize even death in separating them from her. I have twice had instances of vixens carrying away *dead* cubs from discovered dens.

The fox has developed a considerable talent for seeing without being seen and an ability to utilize the apparently scant cover of bare hills to the utmost. In many years on the hill in a calling which demands sharp eyes and keen observation I would guarantee I have been seen by foxes scores of times without seeing them. A fox, snug in deep heather, or ensconced on a sheltered, sun-warmed ledge on a cliff face, will lie tight, confident that he is unseen, and let humans pass by, very closely at times.

This self-confidence, or cunning if you like (though this 'lying tight' is a trait shared by other animals), can at times cause foxes to overreach themselves.

While out stalking hinds one winter my brother Hugh came below, and consequently was overlooked by, a cliff face studded with heather-grown ledges. His path led him up through the cliff and as he gained the top a gust of wind blew his cap off and away it sailed down the cliff face, coming to rest above one of the heathery ledges. Hugh scrambled down, quietly as it happened, to retrieve it and in doing so caught a glimpse of red on the ledge below. Craning cautiously over he had a grandstand view of a handsome dog fox curled comfortably in the heather and still intent on the path along which he'd watched Hugh pass. Had it not been for the fortuitous accident of the cap, that fox would have survived to snigger, unsuspected, at the blindness of the human race.

31

In another instance of this, in which I was personally involved, a dog fox lay all morning comfortably on a sunny ledge in a cairn of rocks, and watched four of us with terriers go by below, and some time later, a noisy Hydro Electric Board vehicle go along the rough Wade's road. On the way back, now on a line just on a level with the cairn, I spotted him, and while my colleagues and their terriers halted at my request, I got down, belly flat, accompanied to my discomfiture by two young terriers, and crawled up a gully and round above the cairn. He was still there, nonchalantly surveying my motionless colleagues, about one hundred and fifty yards below, and their anything but motionless terriers, when I rose to my feet within thirty yards of him. He had time for one glance before he paid full price for the folly of being over-confident at the time when the hill lambs were being born and the rounds of the fox dens were under way.

Although one must admire the beauty, the ability to survive and, at times, the devotion of the fox, one should not lose sight of the fact that it is a predator above all else, and an exceedingly efficient killing machine. Too many, on any particular area of ground, can cause havoc. A single adult fox can exist remarkably well on a multiplicity of small prey throughout spring and particularly summer and to a large extent on carrion in winter and early spring. At breeding time it is a different matter. To a hard-pressed fox, in satisfying the ever-growing appetites of a litter of five cubs, a tight-sitting hen grouse (and her eggs, now doomed never to hatch) a recently born deer calf or roe fawn, and, easiest prey of all, and most plentiful, a new-born lamb, all afford easier prey than a fleet hare or rabbit, even assuming these are present, which they are not in many areas of the West Highlands nowadays.

As an instance of the small pickings a fox without cubs will live on, the stomach of a young barren vixen, which I watched searching the glen banks for mice and the nests of ground-nesting birds very early one June morning, contained two separate age groups of ground-nesting young birds, larks or meadow-pipits, besides the plentiful wing-cases of dung-beetles and a little carrion. A large and portly dog fox also shot very early one morning, in July, had obviously dined remarkably well the previous night. In his bulging stomach were remains of three young grouse, three young larks or meadow-pipits, two voles, the whole of a half-grown rabbit (picked up dead, it had 'fly blow' on one ear) and a red rubber ring used in castrating male lambs.

32

A dog fox, weighing on average 14–15 lb. in the Highlands, showing here a handsome white tag to his tail.
When leaving prey uneaten a fox will usually 'taint' it with his own particular brand.

IX

Red deer stags with their antlers in the full velvet of summer.

The 'knobber' (a year-old staggie) found asleep, while I was going around fox dens.

In the heat of that June day we watched red deer hinds seek solace
at the cooling water of a hill loch.

XI

On one visit, to a buzzard's nest containing one young, the empty nest of a chaffinch lay beside it.

XII

A female common buzzard with her two young, the most usual number of late years (1960s).

Above: A fully fledged young buzzard resting after its first flight from the nest.

Right: The head of a buzzard is rounder and more 'benign' in appearance than that of an eagle.

XIII

Above: The young cuckoo which proved such a provoking subject to photograph.

Left: A close-up of a peregrine falcon, boldness implicit in it; a falcon which usually lays her eggs around mid April in the Highlands.

A hen sparrowhawk feeding her young, exhibiting an obvious
tenderness incongruous in such a fierce looking bird of prey.

XV

A hen kestrel and her eggs, laid in early May. No nest is made
by this species, a hollowed out depression on a cliff ledge being
used instead.

XVI

Another female kestrel with a vole, staple prey of this lovely
little bird of prey.

While on the subject of diet, it may not be generally known that foxes on occasion eject castings, as do birds of prey, but in the case of the fox they are round balls mostly of wool, up to almost the size of a tennis ball. I have seen this only twice, roundish balls of fairly tightly compacted wool, containing grouse claws in one case and smelling strongly and unmistakably of the fox's 'turpentine' taint.

At dens in the West Highlands lambs undeniably are the most apparent prey, and though undoubtedly some are picked up dead in the annual lambing mortality, just as undoubtedly many are killed. Nor does the fox always eschew prey near to his den, as has so often been said. I know of at least three instances where prey, lambs, were killed very close to dens. In one case, which caused a shepherd I knew to inveigh bitterly, twin lambs were killed on two successive nights only three hundred yards from the den, and this was the chief factor in its discovery. Lamb-killing is the real reason why Highland keepers are so relentless in their den rounds throughout April, May and June. Other prey of course features, grouse, moles quite often (and often left to decay if other fare offers) hoodies (taken from traps, perhaps) carrion of deer or ewe; at times a still-born deer calf, and, after mid June, recently born deer calves. Roe deer fawns (only about four pounds in weight at birth) and, at a west coast den, the head of a seal. Remarkable prey here once was a two-pound trout being carried in by a vixen when she was shot.

Like deer-stalking it is often the surroundings in which fox den rounds are pursued that transcend the actual kill. When one adds to this the relative novelty of nights spent out at dens the interest can be keen indeed.

I remember a frosty night spent overlooking Loch Ness, on a steep, rocky hill which at one time held wild goats. Though a dry night it was intensely cold. A velvety, dark-blue canopy sparkled with the silvery brilliance of countless stars, lighting but certainly not warming us. The vixen did appear that night, on a skyline seventy yards from a colleague who swore later, as all of us have done, that he couldn't understand how he had missed her with a 'scope mounted rifle. A fortunate vixen this for running from that shot she almost literally ran over the legs of another helper, to be handsomely missed with both barrels of his shotgun.

The owner of that particular estate was with us that night, and wending our rather heavy-headed way home next morning, through some long, rough heather, he elected, rather prematurely, to unload

33

his gun. From his feet rose a moment or so later a fox, rather draggled looking and with no white tag to the tail, out of range of those of us whose guns were loaded. My colleague's sotto voce language was warming and colourful, but, alas, unprintable. We parted from the owner while he had still half a mile to go to his house, and while still in our view, and still with empty gun, he flushed another fox, this time with a large white tag to the tail. My colleague, whose ground bordered on this estate was by then, perhaps fortunately, speechless.

We had been outsmarted that night, but a year or two later a vixen at a den I'd discovered outsmarted herself, though she was undoubtedly unlucky in doing so.

From my notes: 'I set the rolled-up sleeping bag in a little hollow, overlooking the den but overlooked by a ridge running above it, and began my vigil. The strong westering sun was shining full in my eyes and the opposite face was consequently wrapped in deep shadow, ideal for a fox returning from that direction, to see me while yet unseen. At all events 11.30 p.m. arrived without my seeing a thing, apart from the wafting appearance of a tawny owl in the fading light, which worked along, in silent, eerie flight, from hazel tree to hazel tree below me, perching momentarily in each with a throw-up of silent wings. Needless to surmise what would occur should any roosting bird flutter therein, or any rodent stir in the grass below.

'It was now too dark to shoot except at a skylined target, and as a last resort I left my rolled-up sleeping bag and went down the slope a little to stand now with my back to a spreading alder tree, from which I could command the skylined ridge, eighty yards distant. Hardly had I got there when so quietly and suddenly as to be uncanny in that hushed night, a fox materialized on the skyline, slinking vulpine-like along it, *stalking my rolled-up sleeping bag*. It stopped broadside, peering down at my bag, and I killed it thus, a slim vixen. Undoubtedly she had seen me earlier that night and had later stalked in, in the dusk, for a closer look. Had I not shifted position, unknown to her, she might well have looked her fill and stolen away again, undetected.

A check up on dens in May one year was remarkable in that I stood over a sleeping red deer 'knobber' for ten minutes while I photographed him, all the time managing to restrain, incredibly, a couple of inquisitive terriers without waking the curled-up 'knobber'.

He had been lying with a herd of sixteen deer when I came on them and while the others ran, he slumbered on. A former colleague once stalked and shot a sleeping stag; I did nothing so dastardly, simply shot my 'knobber' on film.

High-ground rounds, of cairns and peat-holes remote from even the houses of stalkers and shepherds, were usually done in June. Late one June evening a colleague arrived to see me and after some preliminary small talk asked if I would go on such a round with him. The area to be searched was exceedingly remote, a good twelve miles from human habitation and at an altitude of 2,500 feet, a high-ground plateau so cut up by burns and peat-hags as to *appear* desolation itself. And yet, in summer this daunting waste is rich in life. Ptarmigan and grouse overlap in nesting on it, with golden plover and dunlin. Meadow-pipits are legion while snipe find its bogs congenial and teal and tufted duck, occasionally a pair of common scoter, favour the small black lochans dotted among its bogs. Greenshank nest sparsely and the eagle glides over it almost daily. For all its forbidding aspect to our eyes, the plateau affords ample feeding in summer and its height and remoteness, guaranteeing peace from tormenting flies and disturbing humans, make it a Mecca for red deer then. Sheep are scarce on it, preferring the larger greens of the lower glen faces. In the drier peat banks of this bogland and in rocky cairns around its edges foxes denned up at times, feeding their cubs on grouse, ptarmigan and fledgeling, ground-nesting birds, on ringousel, wheatear and pipit and, in June, on deer calves.

A ten-mile progression, up General Wade's road (the jolting in my colleague's Land Rover being of that type facetiously described as 'good for the liver') finally saw us at the summit of the road, where it passes over the shoulder of Corrieyairack. Though it was to save us a walk of twenty miles in the day I was glad to be released from the infernal bone-shaking machine at last.

Our first halt was at a huge cairn, a chaotic littering of grey, lichened rocks which filled one side of a small deeply indented pass, just on the march with another estate. The day was now sunny and increasing in warmth. At the cairn we found the bodies of two well-grown cubs, two empty cartridge cases, and a hundred yards farther west a dead dog fox. We had been forestalled, obviously very recently by our neighbours, marching with us on the remote tops but sixty miles around by the road. The story we heard later. A den had been found on their low ground and the vixen and three cubs killed. The

35

dog fox had somehow contrived to get two cubs away and a long
search had culminated in the high ground cairn.

Our way took us east now and on the green face at the end of the
pass a pair of ptarmigan scuttled before us, loath to take wing until the
nearness of our terriers made this imperative. The peat-hags, stretching on all sides now, were alive with deer, lying cudding, on the
'islands' of heather, or cooling off on the damp black of the peat
banks. Seeing us, a trickle of disturbed deer steadily grew until we
had about two hundred crossing ahead of us, the few recently born
calves bleating in shrill falsetto with the deeper lowing call of the
mothers encouraging them on, a cacophony of sound typical of a
disturbed red deer herd at this time of year. The herd halted while
still within spying distance and I watched a yearling feed greedily
from a hind which did not try to evade this 'illicit' feeding. Had she
lost her new calf, and, heavy in milk, was glad to find relief in the
sucking of her previous year's calf?

Moss-hole after moss-hole we tried, in the dry peat-banks, but
without success. At each one my eldest boy, Lea, on holiday from
school, was full of anticipation. Disappointed in this, there was
plenty of other interest to keep him engrossed. In the biggest of the
lochans a hind was standing well out in its cooling waters and as we
watched two others stampeded down through the hags, bucking and
prancing, to splash through the shallows towards her. Away in the
distance a few stags, their new antlers growing thick-looking in
velvet, dotted the haggy ground.

We lunched, boiling eggs and sweet black tea, in smoke-blackened
cans over a heather fire, by the green banks of a burn which mean-
dered across the flat. After this welcome break we arrived, at last, at
the farthest east peat-hole and then turned to work our way home,
thankfully, for the up-and-down going was heavy in the heat of that
day, among the bogs and peat runners of that plateau.

My colleague's indefatigable terrier, fresh from being lured away
from the vicinity of her chicks by a hen grouse, fluttering in con-
vincingly crippled manner, and now out for blood at all costs, found
and grabbed a recently born deer calf whose falsetto bleat brought us
running in time to rescue it. Only hours old, it soon recovered from
its fright and, in fact, attempted to follow us as we left so that we had
to direct my youngster to hold it until we got some way off with the
terriers. Lea then made a successful bolt for it before the calf, still
tottery on its legs, could follow.

36

Though all the known dens were untenanted there were signs of foxes. Occasionally, tracks were seen in the soft moist peat of some of the bogs and once a terrier dug up a distinctly high-smelling grouse chick buried under a scrap of moss, while farther on we found a ravaged grouse nest, with remains of eggs which had obviously been 'hard-set', scattered around.

While yet a mile from our vehicle we had to stage a rescue operation to free a blackface ewe, stuck fast in a quaking bog, onto which tempting green tussocks had lured her. We both sank over the ankles before we freed her, the bog, reluctant to lose its victim, sucking and pulling at her. Touched by her all too obvious weakness, my colleague in a sudden rush of generosity poured a tot of whisky from a flask he carried down her throat.

It was 8.30 p.m. before we reached the Land Rover, and the sharp-fanged top of the hills far away to the west were etched black against a delicate orange glow, a wild, yet tranquil sight to round off a memorable day.

spoke, with an obvious feeling for the young, of a buzzard's nest from which he had shot the hen, and of re-visiting it some days later to find the starving young almost buried in a mess of maggot-infested, putrefying prey, which the cock buzzard was faithfully carrying in but lacked the instinct to feed the young as his dead mate would have done. Of another time, with admiration tinged with regret, of a hen sparrowhawk who persisted in returning to her nest although she had been hit on previous occasions by the waiting keeper. 'She must have been nearly shot to bits,' he said. And again, of finding a merlin's nest, and of going out next day with a colleague to try and shoot the female. Such was the outlook of his generation of keepers and, indeed, estate owners towards birds of prey. We can be thankful that a more sensible attitude of live and let live prevails today, even if before reaching this state of mind we have lost many attractive species. There are undoubtedly still people who will kill, clandestinely, even such largely beneficial species as kestrel and buzzard, but they are in a minority and the danger nowadays is in indirect effects, such as that thought to be due to certain chemical insecticides and seed dressings, rather than from direct persecution.

The name 'common' borne by the buzzard is probably apt over most of the Highlands, though not necessarily throughout Britain. The Scottish Tourist Board might well consider a grant towards the well-being of this bird for it sends many tourists home to the South having 'seen an eagle perched on a telegraph pole'. So often is this said to me that I consider that 'telegraph-pole eagle' might fit as an alternative title for the buzzard. There is, mind you, good excuse for this mistake, for, seen alone, particularly when in flight high above, the buzzard looks majestic enough, lacking anything to give it 'scale'. It would be dwarfed, however, alongside an eagle. Comparative weights of a fully fledged eaglet and a fully fledged young buzzard which I weighed in the same year were $9\frac{3}{4}$ lb. and $1\frac{3}{4}$ lb.

If not quite of eagle status, the buzzard is a handsome bird and its familiar mewing cry is evocative in its wildness. It has a habit of soaring high in lazy spirals and a less apparent one of perching motionless on some strategic watching point for long periods, from where it launches itself upon any prey seen by its keen eye. Its speed in flight does not appear remarkable and I believe it catches the major part of its prey on the ground, by this habit of waiting and watching. I once, admittedly, put a buzzard up from a newly killed wood-pigeon, but I believe this was probably taken by surprise as it fed on the ground, for I cannot believe that the rather lethargic looking buzzard could fly down a wood-pigeon.

In view of the fact that by far the major part of the prey of buzzards consists of rodents and moles the species should be regarded as beneficial, certainly by the farmer. A less endearing habit which buzzards in this area have developed, in the myxomatosis-induced dearth of rabbits, is that of robbing the nests of the smaller birds of their young. Again, this habit of sitting immobile, its brown and white markings blending in well with foliage, enables it to spot parents returning to nests, in feeding young, and, having located the nest, the next step is to filch the young to feed its own young. The most revealing instance I have noted of this was the finding of an empty nest of a chaffinch, lying on a buzzard's nest, the erstwhile occupants presumably inside the young buzzard which stood beside it.

What never ceases to astonish me is that the buzzard *did* survive the persecution era when so many related species did not. It is easily trapped or shot and it builds a very obvious, bulky nest high in a tree, often before the trees are in full leaf. It will also use a cliff site and, while a site of that nature is less obvious, even in this case the bulk of the nest and the fact that the parents *will* circle above, mewing their alarm, whenever one is near a nest, often gives the site away. The buzzard is also notorious for deserting its nest, particularly if disturbed before the eggs hatch, and when this happens, seldom, if ever, lays a second clutch. There is, too, the fact that the buzzard seems very vulnerable to predation on its eggs, or young, by other nest-robbers, notably the hooded crow. I have known of eggs sucked and left empty, on a tree nest; of two out of three chicks to vanish from another, while a nestful of young hoodies waxed fat, until I found them, only three hundred yards distant, and of the two chicks of a cliff eyrie to disappear. In the case of cliff sites I believe the agile stoat could well be the predator on occasion where young disappear.

One may feel this is no more than just retribution in view of the buzzards' killing of fledgelings, in the nest or while still at the fluttery, learning-to-fly stage. Be that as it may, despite all these apparent drawbacks to its survival, survive it has, nor does it seem to have been as hard hit by pesticides as eagle, peregrine falcon or sparrowhawk. A factor which may have helped to ensure the buzzard's survival is that attribute which it shares with other 'successful' species, such as fox or hoodie, namely, its catholic taste in prey. In watching buzzard's nests over the last decade I have noted

41

that the range of prey has been wide and remarkably varied, and includes carrion. The taste for carrion is repulsive to us but it seems a valuable attribute when live prey becomes suddenly scarce, as happened with rabbits and myxomatosis. The buzzard relied heavily on young rabbits when rearing young and in the days when rabbits were plentiful clutches of four eggs were not uncommon, while nowadays clutches of two are the normal. I have twice seen clutches of four raised (the last one in '63) and there is no doubt that such a clutch must test the buzzards' hunting ability to the utmost. With such a clutch the young fledge and leave the nest at intervals, so that the eldest or most forward may have left some days before the last to fly. In such cases I suspect that the last to leave may be neglected by the parents, so far as feeding goes, which have to cope with the constant importuning of three larger young, now on the wing but not yet skilful in finding prey. In the 1963 nest, while I was visiting daily, I helped to rear, perhaps even ensured the survival of, the last to leave, for, noting its ravenous condition in the days after its nest-mates had flown, I used to bring prey for it, a dead rat, or young rabbit, or bird killed on the road, and give this to it. So tame did it get that when, on one or two occasions, I found it perched on a branch *below* the nest, it would jump onto my extended arm and sit there until I put it off onto the nest to feed it.

In 1962 I watched a nest which was so near my house that I was able to visit it daily, making forty-three consecutive visits in all. Over that period, from when the young were a day or two old until the survivor flew, young rabbits and moles were the staple prey. Voles were not seen as often as I'd expected, but these are apparently sweet and tender fare to the young and were eaten very quickly, whereas moles were often left if other fare offered. An interesting, if gruesome, fact was that of five frogs seen as prey three were actually alive on the nest, presumably to be eaten alive in due course. Except that is the one which I extricated from below the young buzzard, who appeared to be brooding it, and which jumped into space from off the nest, preferring, apparently, suicide to being swallowed alive.

This nest contained two young but at three weeks old the weaker of the two succumbed to the almost constant bullying of the larger one, its head, when I found it dead, a mass of bloodstained cuts. This is the only instance of this kind I have so far noted in buzzards.

In all the forty-three days I was able only twice to approach the

42

nest without an adult 'mewing' above. It appeared that the vantage point of a tall oak tree on the bank of the glen opposite the nest was used as a lookout by whichever of the pair was not on hunting duty. Buzzards share with eagles the habit of freshening their nests with greenery periodically, throughout the fledging time. That particular pair seemed to have a definite eye for décor, for whereas at former nests I watched mainly birch and rowan sprays were brought in, at this one sprays of birch, rowan, oak, hazel, ash, elm, alder and ivy were used. From observations made from a hide it seemed invariably the female who provided the décor. On one occasion the adult pair arrived together, the cock with a vole in his beak, the hen with a small spray of oak. Small prey, voles and moles, etc., were carried in the beak, larger prey, as young rabbits, were carried in the talons of one foot. Prey noted over the fledging period was as under: Rabbit (all young ones), thirty-two times, with moles next in frequency, nineteen times (seven adult, twelve young), five frogs (three alive), four voles, three fledgeling thrushes, two fledgeling robins, one fledgeling dipper, one snipe (found dead?), the highly odorous remains of a black-headed gull, one fledgeling cuckoo and lamb carrion on five occasions. The lamb carrion was, I suspect, scavenged from a fox den high on the opposite side of the hill and the remains of the gull may also have come from there.

At the 1963 nest, visited thirty-nine times throughout the fledging period, the parents had to work really hard to feed the four young. One of the four was very markedly smaller than the others yet it suffered no persecution. At this nest prey noted was as under. Twenty-four young rabbits, eight voles, four moles, carrion on three occasions and once the afterbirth of a lambing ewe. Feathered prey was more in evidence at this nest than usual; three fledgeling robins, two fledgeling blackbirds, and once each, wood-pigeon, jackdaw, cuckoo, oyster-catcher, grouse and a very young mallard duckling still clad in dirty-grey down.

It will be noted that rabbit was the main prey in '62 and '63. These were years in which the rabbit had made a temporary comeback. However, the vile scourge of myxomatosis recurred, or more likely was illegally re-introduced, and once more scythed down the rabbit population. Very different, therefore, was the prey situation in 1967 at a nest visited on fifty-four successive occasions: here, a young rabbit appeared only *once*, though to make up for this moles numbered thirty-nine, and fledgeling small birds were noted on

43

twenty-seven occasions, including thrush, blackbird, robin, redstart, chaffinch and yellow-hammer. It was at this nest that the empty chaffinch nest was seen. Other prey consisted, remarkably, of two hoodies (probably juveniles barely able to fly, but completely fledged), and, less remarkably, seven voles, one frog, one brown rat, one shrew, two mice, one toad and one beetle. The young bird was on the nest from hatching at 29th May until flying on 22nd July.

Many people have expressed wonder at the apparent ease with which the buzzard catches moles. I have no doubt but that the sitting and waiting tactics of the buzzard are employed in this, too, and wherever a mole surfaces, which they may do oftener than most people suspect, the buzzard pounces.

While to see a buzzard is a daily commonplace event in the Highlands, to see the peregrine falcon, that superlative flyer and scourge of a wide variety of bird-life from carrier pigeon to ptarmigan, is a rare and memorable event. I remember seeing one, flying fast over a wide glade, reach forward in full flight and delicately scratch below its 'chin' with one extended foot, and another, an immature bird, perched like a graven image on a fence post, well out on the hill, so that one almost passed it over as an extension of the post. Most memorable, however, was the time I witnessed a peregrine kill a grouse, high above me. I was hind-stalking at the time and was sitting, in snow, clad in my winter whites for camouflage, watching some deer. Above me, suddenly, I heard a harsh peregrine-chortle (of satisfaction, I now assume) and looked up in time to see a peregrine bind to a grouse; nothing very spectacular, no air-rending stoop or resounding impact, no headless grouse hurtling earthwards, the only sound that harsh 'chortle'. Still rapidly flying away from me, a momentary struggle was obvious, with the grouse held so close up to the falcon's breast as to be almost indistinguishable. And then the grouse dropped limply to the full extent of the falcon's legs and she flew round, heavily burdened, in a wide semi-circle, getting lower and lower, to land only about two hundred yards from where I crouched, spellbound. There she stood, atop the grouse, wings half extended over it, her head up, looking imperiously around, the snowy back-cloth rendering every detail clear. Quite suddenly and altogether unexpectedly, she took wing and left it, for no apparent reason. I gave her some time but she did not reappear and so I went over to the dead grouse, lying on its back, wings out and with its head hidden in the soft snow. A deep laceration slowly reddening the snow was, I believe, caused by the initial attack of the falcon, and underneath the wing as it was, at the junction of wing and body, it must have immediately crippled the grouse. The *coup de grâce* which I believe I had witnessed in the momentary mid-air struggle had been with the beak, a severing of the neck's vertebrae.

Peregrines take possibly the widest range of feathered prey (and this almost all on the wing) of all our native raptors. They will, however, occasionally, take prey from the ground, for I have seen vole fur in castings at an eyrie and once saw a ptarmigan chick, scarcely hatched, brought in.

I spent a very interesting time one year watching an eyrie which held two young. The peregrine does not 'make' a nest, she will simply hollow out a depression in the soil of a cliff ledge and lay her eggs, usually four, in this, or, a popular choice, take over the disused nest of a raven, a bird which favours the same sort of nasty cliffs as she does. On this occasion the huge eyrie of a golden eagle was used and the four eggs which lay on it looked ludicrously tiny in its immensity. The young, only two from four eggs, hatched about 20th May and I toiled up the steep face to the eyrie a day or so later, reaching it, to my surprise, without the harsh screeching protest by one or both adults which usually occurs when anyone is within a half-mile of a peregrine's eyrie. Craning cautiously forward over the cliff top above the nest I saw the falcon sitting, about fifteen feet below me, the slaty, blue-grey of her back feathers ruffled in the strong breeze. Her darker head turned this way and that as she brooded, until, suddenly and telepathically aware of my scrutiny she twisted her head right round, owlwise, and looked straight up at me. At once she took wing, shrieking harshly with that grating, rusty-hinge cry of the affronted peregrine. Gaining altitude rapidly she went into a vertical, tremendously fast, stoop at me, pulling out with a very audible 'swoosh' about twenty yards up. These tactics she kept repeating while I looked at her two chicks, fragile-looking morsels of white down with pink flesh showing through, and shell-pink, almost translucent-looking, beaks. High above, the tiercel had also arrived, but beyond some harsh screeching in moral support, he took no part in the falcon's intimidatory stoops. Feathers of pigeon, oyster-catcher and kestrel lay on the eyrie. I had seen feathers of a kestrel below a peregrine eyrie on a previous occasion and it seems that on occasion predator will eat predator.

On 30th May I found evidence of the size of prey a peregrine will

45

tackle in the shape of a part-eaten curlew lying at the loch-side below the eyrie. The neck was completely broken, the head twisted round backwards, while the body was almost completely plucked but the wings still completely feathered. Only the back had been eaten; the breast, to us the choicer part, was untouched. At the eyrie the two young, still down-clad, were lying amidst feathers of cuckoo, jackdaw and grouse, evidence of a varied diet. The following week-end the eyrie was bare of prey signs and the young, while still down-clad, were now sitting up and taking notice, instead of sleeping nearly all day. I was just about to leave when one of the adults came flying fast and direct to the eyrie, a small yellowish object dangling in one foot. Seeing me, it really 'stood on the brakes' and seemed to rise and turn in the one motion, dropping the prey, invariable reaction in a startled raptor, as it did so. Curious as to what it was, thinking in terms of yellow-hammer or grey wagtail, I *searched for an hour* before I found it in the long heather into which it had dropped. It was neither yellow-hammer nor wagtail but the ptarmigan chick already alluded to.

At four weeks old the first feathering became apparent on the two youngsters and they were now active and strong on their legs, the long middle talon of the falcon foot almost like a deformity in comparison to the other talons. The eyrie was now a charnel-house, for the falcon disdains the greenery décor of eagle and buzzard. Evident were the remains of oyster-catcher, carrier-pigeon, grouse and golden plover.

On my way home that day I found a nearly-fledged young cuckoo, filling, indeed squashing out of shape, a meadow-pipit's nest. A most ugly fledgeling to my eyes, adopting a threatening, bullying attitude, incongruous in something so small and helpless, its wide-open gape a striking orange-red in colour.

The young peregrines were half fledged at five weeks old. A webbed foot, from gull or tern it seemed, lay beside a grouse claw and some pigeon feathers. The falcon stooped repeatedly on me that day, with a tearing, explosive displacement of air as she pulled out above me. As with a minority of the eagles I had studied, the falcon seemed to become more aggressive as the young grew older. They, for their part, kept up an incessant nerve-fraying screeching, verging on hysteria it seemed at times, and the bolder of the two scuttled across the eyrie at me two or three times and clutched at my hand.

The young cuckoo I had found the previous week had outgrown

its foster-nest and was now hunched up beside it. It again kept up a continual threat display, head, crop and indeed all of its body feathers fluffed out in comical blown-out fashion and deep orange-red gape wide open. Puffing itself up and down in a perpetual jack-in-the-box motion it was infuriatingly disconcerting to photograph.

Six weeks after hatching the young peregrines were fully fledged, with only stray, thistledown wisps of down showing through the dark-brown back and wing feathers of the immature plumage. Both parents stunted and screeched above as I approached, and as if in answer to exhortation, one of the young began screeching as soon as I appeared, and, still screeching, flew off the eyrie and round a ridge out of sight. Its nest mate elected to retire to the back of the eyrie instead of taking wing and I took a last photograph and left. Prey remains littered the eyrie that day, of grouse, pigeon, teal, sandpiper and ring-ouzel. It was obvious that the eyrie would be empty by the following week-end and so I did not return. An interesting six weeks had passed in which the wide variety of peregrine prey had been made manifest to me.

A much smaller bird of prey yet every whit as dashing as the peregrine is the sparrowhawk. Though I cannot but admire the piratical, rakish dash of this hawk it is actually the bird of prey I like least, simply because I once surprised a hen sparrowhawk plucking *alive* a shrieking blackbird, presumably as a prelude to eating it alive. The sparrowhawk looks incredibly swift as it dashes in pursuit of its prey and is extremely single-minded in this. I have had one crash into our living-room window in pursuit of a blackbird. I retrieved the stunned bird and found it uninjured except for one neat talon-puncture. It recovered sufficiently to fly away later. I have also watched a sparrowhawk hotly pursue a wheatear across a glen and catch it, plucking it out of mid-air expertly. My older son, Lea, has been lucky enough to see one dash into a flock of redwings and retire with its shrieking prey, while my younger son, Michael, has seen a swallow taken in mid-air. As to bigger prey, prey indeed, as big as herself (and the hen sparrowhawk is *markedly* larger than the cock) I have noted wood-pigeon, and on reliable eye-witness report, a lapwing, from the warm corpse of which my informant put up a hen sparrowhawk. However, watching nests in an attempt to find out the prey, disclosed small finch-size birds as the overwhelming majority brought in to feed the young.

47

Sparrowhawks do not lay their eggs until May, but the nest is often built weeks before the eggs are laid. I witnessed a nest completed in March one year, and waited and waited for the bird to lay, thinking, at last, that she had deserted the nest. But no, she laid five handsome chalky-green eggs blotched with red-brown markings, in May, and reared three young to flying stage.

The sparrowhawk, unlike the peregrine, does build a nest, and I have always found the nests in birch trees, and always made of birch twigs. The nest is a wide, flat platform of birch twigs with a very shallow cup in its centre. No lining whatever is used, unless one can call the interlacing of very thin birch twigs which forms the shallow cup, a lining. So shallow is the central cup that I always wondered that the eggs were not rolled 'overboard', whenever the hen left the nest. In one year I did see a chick knocked onto the outer edge of the nest when the hen sparrowhawk left it. She came back almost immediately and I then witnessed her—to our way of thinking— incredible stupidity or insensitivity, for she lighted on the nest and shuffled the young in the cup below her breast and settled down to brood them. The almost evicted chick was struggling on the nest edge, and calling feebly, within *inches* of her head. Once she cocked her head sideways and looked at it but she took no further notice and a moment or so later the chick fell off. It would have been so easy for her, a bird used to employing her beak in dealing with prey, to have pulled her chick back into the cup and below her breast with the others.

At a nest I watched one year the hen laid her first egg on 7th May and from the four eggs of her completed clutch she hatched three young on 22nd June. From this she reared only two, the third being the victim of the mishap mentioned above. For the first seven days or so the hen brooded the young constantly and at this stage the cock did all the hunting, giving a high-pitched 'food-call' as he came by the nest on his way to his plucking stool so that the hen was all expectancy, as, minutes later, plucking completed, he bore the denuded victim into the nest. In feeding the young, on tiny morsels picked from the prey, this was proffered to them on her beak, from which they pecked it: that is, they were not fed by stuffing food *into* their beaks, they had the active part *of taking it* themselves from the hen's beak. Her mien on these occasions was almost unbelievably tender in so fierce-looking a hawk as she patiently offered the titbits until the young were full-fed, when she usually ate the rest for herself.

That most strikingly beautiful bird of our Highland hill lochs, the
black-throated diver, on her nest.

In her nest, little more than a depression, the black-throated
diver arranged her egg to her satisfaction before sitting on it.
It is elongated, dark olive-brown, sparsely blotched with black.

The redwing, showing plainly its distinctive light eye stripe.

The redwing at her nest on an upturned birch root. These photographs are probably the first taken of a British breeding redwing.

Above and upper right: Feeding her four expectant young with earth-worms, which formed the staple prey.

XXI

Right: Removing an ejected capsule of excrement from one of her young.

XX

XXII The greenshank, one of our most interesting waders which choose, surprisingly, to nest on the high ground peaty plateaus in the Highlands; and the four lovely plover-like eggs.

A ptarmigan, exposed on a ridge of the high tops, obvious appearing, and in contrast among the grey rocks into which these birds of the high hills blend so superlatively.   XXIII

Ptarmigan chicks, newly hatched, 'delightfully fluffy yellow balls', in their nest on the high ground.

XXIV

I should explain here that watching the actual *nest* of a sparrow-hawk in an effort to study the prey brought in, is most unrewarding, for all prey is plucked and decapitated when it arrives. Near to every nest is a 'plucking stool', a spur of rock, a tree-stump or something similar to which the sparrowhawk brings its prey to pluck before taking it to the nest. It is *here* that one can gain a good idea of the prey being brought in, by the feathers scattered around, though it is advisable to collect these on each visit so as to have fresh ones to identify.

Feeding times, when the chicks were a few days old, were at about three-hourly intervals, and in feeding them the hen ate the 'coarser' parts, like legs and wings. On the very infrequent occasions in that first seven days when the hen was absent on the cock's arrival at the nest he simply dropped the prey and flew away at once. His role, as with other birds of prey, was that of the hunter only. Once the chicks were over a week old the cock came round much less frequently to the nest; instead, his usual food call as he passed the nest brought the hen to the plucking stool where, presumably, she took delivery of the prey. The cock sparrowhawk was an exceedingly dapper little bird, much smaller and less fierce-looking than his mate, vivid in slate-blue and chestnut red, contrasting with her overall soft-grey appearance. As the chicks grew older both parents shared the hunting to feed the rapidly growing young. At three weeks old the young were half-fledged and beginning to pick at the prey for themselves, although the hen continued to feed them.

On 16th July one of the young, still not fully fledged, was perched on a branch on the nest tree and flew away as I arrived. The hen came in later and fed the remaining young one and herself, in alternate morsels, on the prey she brought in. After she left the young one did some comical, half-hopping, half-flying exercises around the nest, followed by a preening session, which caused bits of down to float lazily away in the still air, some of it to be ensnared in the surrounding twigs. By 21st July both young were flying, but continued to use the nest as a 'dining-table', on hearing the parents' food call as prey was brought in. At no time during this nesting period did I see prey larger than thrush-size brought in and indeed, in July, it seemed to consist mainly of fledgelings.

The kestrel, that lovely red-brown hoverer, tied to the 'ceiling' of the sky by some invisible thread as it hovers, motionless except for rapidly beating wings, over the one spot, dipping suddenly lower, to hover again, while it watches for vole, lizard or even beetle in the heather below is, up here, a cliff-nester. Like the peregrine it makes no nest, but lays four or five handsome, red-brown eggs in a shallow hollow excavated in a cliff-ledge. The eggs are usually laid about the same time as the sparrowhawk's and the young have a similar fledging period. Like young sparrowhawks, they too, will fly before being fully-fledged. Prey I have seen at nests has been overwhelmingly of vole, with lizard, frog and mole featuring and, occasionally, meadow-pipit. A laughable sight I saw one year at a nest I was watching was of a nearly fledged young kestrel with a huge drooping moustache below its beak. As I drew nearer I saw the moustache to be the two massive, digger 'hands' of a mole. Even as I watched, the young kestrel disgorged almost the entire skin of the mole, all of which it had got down, except the front feet. Time after time, it tried to get it down but it always ended in frustration and the comical moustachioed appearance.

I have never, unfortunately, found the nest of a merlin and indeed, have only rarely seen this tiny hawk. It is certainly very much scarcer in this area than any of the foregoing species. Perhaps some day I may have the luck to photograph this bird, and study the prey brought in to its nest.

5

Hill Loch to High Tops

ONE of the charms of the Highland scene lies in the numerous hill lochs which lend diversity and attraction to terrain which might otherwise be a monotone of heather and rock. These lochs also attract bird-life which might otherwise be absent. Diver, grebe and goosander, mallard, teal and tufted duck, reed-bunting and sand-piper bring variety to the birds of mountain and moorland.

The most strikingly handsome of the species which come to our hill lochs to breed are, in my estimation, the black-throated divers, birds which lend distinction to any loch they grace with their presence. This diver is the epitome of sleek grace on water, but para-doxically an ungainly, lurching feathered caricature on land. Supremely fitted for its aquatic existence, coming on land only to nest, the diver's long, streamlined body, with its widely webbed foot set very far back on it, make it a figure of fun on land. Quite unable to balance in walking upright, it must grovel grotesquely forward, pushed by its webbed feet, when coming ashore to nest. The plumage is a study in black, white and dove-grey, with an elegant streamlined svelteness almost unreal in quality. I have never seen a diver with ruffled feathers, indeed, the sleek sheen of the plumage, particularly of head and neck, gives me the impression of velvet pile rather than of feathers. In length it is twenty-three inches to twenty-seven inches, rather larger than a mallard drake.

Relatively scarce, its numbers are probably largely dictated by its nesting and habitat requirements, that is, a hill loch of a fair size with, preferably, at least one island suitable for nesting purposes. This island, to be suitable, must have at least one stretch of shore which shelves very gradually from the water's edge for if it is steep-banked the diver just cannot get up it because of its awkwardly placed legs. Usually, the nest will be as close to the water's edge as possible. At one nest I watched the bird had to shovel itself, breast ploughing up the sand, up a gradually shelving beach for some six feet; at another nest, a heave up out of the water and she was almost at the nest. The diver at the first nest had to adopt the same shovelling, laborious progress back to the water when leaving the nest; at the second, one heave of the webbed feet sent the diver off the nest and head-first into the loch which, in this case, deepened abruptly about a foot from the shore. In this spectacular departure the bird dived at once, and did not surface until many yards out on the loch.

A migrant, the black-throated diver winters along the sea coasts, and I usually see my first birds inland around the third week in April, not always on their nesting loch but sometimes resting on a loch en route to the breeding one. A memorable view through my stalking 'glass' in one year, on 22nd April, was of three black-throated divers, far out on Loch Garry, on a day of glorious sunshine which had the waters of the loch blue and sparkling. The divers cruised contentedly around, conspicuous in black, white and grey and sometimes rose erect, on 'tip-toe', to beat their wings vigorously before subsiding on to the blue water again. On another occasion in early June I watched three divers, this time on a breeding loch, cruising around unhurriedly in arrowhead formation. At times one or other would dive, leaving two on the surface to cruise on, yet the submerged bird would always surface in exactly its former place in the formation. Sometimes all three would be cruising along, all apparently headless, with necks extended ahead of them at water level and heads totally submerged as they searched the depths below, reminding me irresistibly of a skin diver swimming flat on the surface, with his glass eyepiece scanning the underwater world.

On a breeding loch known to me the diver was unsuccessful over a two-year period, during which she nested on the same spot on the same island on this loch. In the first year, I saw her sitting from the shore, and rowed over to investigate. She had not yet laid (22nd May) but on the most easterly point of the island, had formed a wide, shallow depression, rather more luxuriantly lined, with dried rush stems, than is usual. She did lay in due course but on revisiting the

52

nest in June I found it empty. I suspected human agency but could not verify this.

The following year she laid two eggs on exactly the same spot, only to have them both smashed by a heavy-footed, adventurous black-face ewe in scrambling ashore after swimming across to the island, over the narrow but deep channel which separated island from mainland. Probably the tempting green of the island, well fertilized by generations of common gulls, lured the ewe across for a sweet bite. Roe deer also have been seen swimming across to this island, similarly lured.

In the third year, on 2nd June I saw the diver sitting at the usual nest-site while the cock floated discreetly in the background of the loch. A few days later I set out at 4.30 a.m. and rowed across to the small wooded island, heralded by raucous outcry from the gulls. The cock was out on the loch and dived when he saw me and, when he surfaced, contrived to keep incredibly flat, looking round furtively meantime. Alarmed, undoubtedly, by the gulls' outcry there was no diver on the nest when I arrived. This time the single, large egg, curiously shaped, long, and with both ends 'blunt' (i.e. neither end tapered off) lay simply in a shallow depression within feet of the water, without any attempt at nesting materials. In colour it was a dark olive brown, sparsely blotched with black. I hastily put up a few birch branches between two convenient birch trees, about fifteen feet from the nest, and left the island. While I worked both divers kept an eye on me from out on the loch, riding buoyantly about one hundred and fifty yards away. Before I left I made sure that the diver had returned to her egg, that my rough hide, of natural, on-the-spot materials hadn't alarmed her.

Some ten days later I again went to the loch, at around 7.0 a.m. to await the arrival of my brother, Hugh, who was going to row me over to the island, put me into my hide, cover me with some more natural camouflage of heather and moss, and then leave me to my own devices. There were no fewer than five divers afloat on the loch that morning, floating serenely, quite near the edge, a striking sight in the early morning calm. Before Hugh arrived four of them had left, flying above me, presumably returning to their breeding lochs, leaving the mate of the sitting diver in possession of 'his' loch. Around 8 a.m. Hugh arrived and we rowed across, accompanied by the usual raucous gull outcry, which again put the diver off her eggs. After settling me into my rather cramped quarters, with cameras

53

loaded with monochrome and colour, he departed and I was left viewing through my leafy screen the two divers, riding far out on the loch. I took my eyes off them to set up my cameras and when I next looked only an empty expanse of loch met my eyes.

A few minutes elapsed, then both divers appeared in my restricted frontal view, only a few feet from the nest on the island's tip. The cock was obviously convoying his mate to the nest. They swam past, however, up and down the channel twice before the hen appeared, alone, furtive-looking among the rushes at the islands' edge, to heave herself clumsily on shore and with a couple of flopping movements, up to her egg. She first arranged the egg to her satisfaction (an invariable occurrence with the divers I have watched), and then, thankfully (one almost imagined a sigh of relief), she subsided on to it. At first she sat facing me, just as she came out of the loch, a bead or two of moisture gleaming silvery on her white breast, her beautifully sleek, dove-grey head as immaculate as usual, the wine-red eye gleaming as the light caught it. She soon changed her position to broadside on, then to facing the loch, ready for a speedy withdrawal if necessary, to the safety of its waters.

Though becoming increasingly cramped I enjoyed my vigil; studying a beautiful bird at close range, while quite unsuspected, never palls. A common sandpiper stole the stage at intervals, flitting about with a conspiratorial air between my hide and the diver. Once I watched it stalk an insect, a stealthy 'cat and mouse' approach which resulted in a successful snapping of its prey.

The diver left the nest for a third time about 3 p.m. as gull clangour again waxed loud, and I seized the opportunity to slip out of my hide and shift my paraphernalia to the farther end of the island. I then retraced my steps to the narrow channel at the nest end and swam for the mainland, with little of the diver's assurance or elegance in the water. I landed, I assure you, thankfully, for the channel which looked so narrow seemed inexplicably to widen and the water had become choppy in the strengthening wind.

It only remained to get around the loch's edge to the boat and row across for my gear still on the island, and a most enjoyable session was over.

The diver nested successfully this time and the pair were later to be seen accompanied on the loch by their small sooty-black chick. Zealous parents, they refused to dive or swim fast away while the chick was small but kept within reach all the time. I last saw them on

54

26th July that year, on a most lovely summer evening, cruising across the serene loch, its waters reflecting the rose-tinted cloud of the evening sky. Behind the two adults swam their three-quarters grown young one, a fitting last look at these beautiful birds.

It was in May 1968 that Michael, my youngest son, came home full of excitement with the claim that he and Seamus (my brother's eldest son) had found, in a high-ground birch wood, the nest of a redwing. I threw cold water on his excitement right away. Redwings, charming thrushes with a prominent light eye-stripe and rust-red patches on their flanks, flock to this country each winter from Scandinavia, and while they have attempted, usually unsuccessfully, in very sparse numbers, to breed in the Highlands since the early 1920s I could not believe that we had the luck to have a nest in our area. I checked up for myself, and then had to eat the most humble of pies; it was indisputably a redwing's nest, built mainly of dried grass, very akin to that of the blackbird and on a rather similar site, the upturned root of a fallen birch tree. There were four eggs, rather smaller than those of song-thrush or blackbird; their colour was 'blackbird green', however, thickly dotted with red-brown at the larger end. The hen perched anxiously on a nearby birch, giving me every chance to identify her, showing her eye-stripe and lovely rust-red blush on her flanks below her wing's lower edge. The cock, typically, stayed at a safer distance, 'chack-chacking' in scolding alarm. This was the ornithological event of the year for me.

When the eggs had hatched a hide was made, well camouflaged with natural materials, its construction watched by both parents, anxious, with worms in their beaks, to feed the young. Within ten minutes of its completion, and my withdrawal to a discreet distance, the hen was back to the nest and feeding the young, quite undisturbed by the new large and mossy stump near her nest. Towards the end of May I had a fascinating two hours' vigil in the hide, when the young were about nine days old, taking what may well prove to be the first *British* photographs of a *breeding* redwing. The young were then filling the nest, their heads very dark-looking and with 'ear-tufts' of orange-brown, somnolent for most of the time until the arrival of the hen brought all four heads up, eager for food. This she brought in every ten minutes or so, mainly earth-worms, a tangled cluster in her beak, practically always coming in from the same direction and perching on a root below the nest before fluttering up to the eagerly waiting young, who all had expectant orange-red

55

gapes yawning wide for the worms. As soon as she rid herself of the food, thrusting it down one or two of the gaping gullets so would one of the nestlings, as if by reflex action, rear up an almost naked pink rump and eject a 'capsule-enclosed' white dropping which was immediately seized by the hen. Mostly she carried this away, but on three occasions she swallowed it herself before flying off. Twice during my two-hour watch she fed 'grit' to the young, pecking sandy soil from the upturned root at the back of the nest.

Reliable sources later on that year informed me that there had been an unprecedented number of reports of redwings breeding, so that 1968 may well go down in ornithological circles as the 'redwing year', when these birds first really established themselves as a breeding species here.

Scarcely less exciting was the discovery, or rather the stumbling upon, of another nest, that of a greenshank, one day in early June, as I went, accompanied by a friend and my two sons, Lea and Michael, over to check up on an eagle's eyrie. The greenshank is a relatively scarce and localized breeder in the Highlands, rather similar, though smaller and lacking the down-curved bill, to the curlew. The plumage as the bird flies ahead is predominantly grey, with a very distinct white rump patch. The legs, as one might expect from its name are olive green. Its nest is notoriously difficult to locate.

From my notes then: 'Reaching the high, peaty plateau at the top I was striding it out when a flicker of wings sounded low and behind me, and, simultaneously a delighted shout from Michael (next in line behind) halted me in my tracks. *A greenshank's nest!* And I had walked past within a foot of it without the bird stirring, but the other three coming behind had been too much for her. Four very lovely eggs, a delicate shade of olive green barely tinting their stone ground colour, blotched with dark brown with some underlying delicate lavender markings. We admired, wondered at, and photographed— and hugged ourselves in sheer delight before carrying on to the eyrie, where we found the eaglet flourishing. On our way back we came to the nest very carefully, and sure enough the greenshank was sitting. Knowing of their reputation for "sitting tight" I gradually edged in, hardly daring to breathe, and took some photos at close range and without a telephoto lens. I could hardly wait to develop these but they turned out very well, both in colour and monochrome.'

Perhaps not quite so exciting, as rarity went, but every whit as satisfying in the beauty of the subject was the photograph of a ptarmigan's nest, on a high ridge at the 2,500 feet level. I had almost tripped over the tight-sitting hen (it has been averred that a hen ptarmigan once sat tight between the four legs of a pony until a strap of its harness fell across her back) before I saw her and cautiously shrank backward to get my cameras ready. Here again it was not necessary to use a telephoto lens, the hen sat tight and allowed a series of photos to be taken at close range. She was very hard to detect, in her superb camouflage of delicate greys, browns and whites even although the nest was quite innocent of any cover whatsoever. Her clutch of eight eggs hatched on 19th June and I was lucky enough to be there, lucky because the young of game birds usually leave the nest within hours of hatching so that it is very rare to get a chance to photograph them in the nest. The hen was still sitting tight and I had some difficulty re-locating her. The cock rose from a jumble of grey rock where he had been almost invisible and did his best to draw me away but I was having none of it. I found and photographed the hen and as I did so saw by the way she was sitting that she must have hatched. Even as I watched she was involuntarily 'heaved' upwards by the restless brood below her. When she came off I saw that the chicks were indeed hatched, delightful fluffy, yellow balls marked with red-brown and chocolate-brown. I had then to cope with the rather comical situation of trying to photograph them while the top-most 'layer' strove to burrow below the other chicks, and having achieved this were immediately heaved to the top again and the jockeying for the warmth of the lower layer resumed. While I watched, one chick reached forward to a breast feather of the hen, left on the edge of the nest, and swallowed it. Photographs taken, I left quickly so that the hen could return. When I next visited the nest it was empty, only the hatched-off shells marking its recent occupancy.

6

On the June Hills

EARLY June in the Highlands is a glorious time to be alive and on the hill. The daylight hours are long, the weather usually fairly good, and the trees in the river glens are still fresh in their new green garments, without, yet, that suffocating heaviness of foliage and undergrowth which high summer brings. These same glens are alive with the songs and movements of birds, all engrossed in the annual reproduction of the species, while on the hills meadow-pipits rise at every step and grouse, golden plover and ptarmigan all have family cares to absorb them. The greener hill-faces are painted with flowers, the purples of vetch, yellows of birds-foot trefoil, reds of wild thyme and blues of milkwort, vying with the quieter hues of alpine lady's mantle, lady's bedstraw and mountain everlasting.

It is at this time that the new calves are born to the deer herds each year, for while a very few early calves may come in late May and a few very late ones in July and even August, June is *the* calving month and the month in which the arduous, stamina-testing but intensely interesting research work of ear-tagging red deer calves takes place.

The ear-tagging is still, relatively speaking, in its infancy. The Nature Conservancy began in 1957 on Rhum, the Red Deer Commission in 1963 in Ross-shire, and the Forestry Commission in 1965 in Galloway. I also began in 1965, on Culachy.

Ear-marking is done so that, from recoveries of dead animals and sightings of live animals, the movements and habits of hill deer can be studied. In the dead animal body weights and antler growth (in stags) can be checked relative to *known* age, and also wear on the molars can be similarly checked. It is known that it is possible to estimate fairly closely the age of red deer by the wear on their cheek molars, and by retaining the lower jaws, which include their molars, of animals whose age is known, a series of 'known-age' jaws can eventually be built up as a rule-of-thumb guide to the age of deer in that area. There are many things in red deer life still rather obscure to us in the Highlands and ear-marking is one method by which we can replace surmise with fact. An indirect aspect of ear-marking is that one learns much by direct observation at this time in being, necessarily, on the hill for much of the daylight hours in June.

The actual tagging operation is simple enough. Suitable ear-tags are bought, of metal or, as I prefer, plastic roto tags, with the 'pliers' for attaching these. It has been found, however, that the metal tags which clamp on the ear are more permanent than the plastic tags, which can on occasion be lost by the marked animal. The disadvantage of the metal tags is that they soon become indistinguishable in the live animal so that future data is available only from the dead beast. Plastic tags come in a variety of bright colours and can be distinguished, even at some distance, on the living animal, thus affording recognition of the tagged animal and data from the living beast. An even more advanced method is the use of individually-coloured, durable plastic 'flashes', behind the actual tag. Using different colours, or even combinations of colours, one is then able to identify from a distance individual living animals which is of great value in tracing movements, etc.

Whatever tags one uses they should be inscribed with the year (i.e., '67' for '1967'), a code name for the estate (i.e. 'Cul' for 'Culachy') and be numbered successively. Ideas of application may vary, whether to attach them to different ears according to sex, or to do as I did, having two distinct herds, attach to the left ear for one herd and to the right ear for the other. For the actual application the calf is held between the legs of the tagger and the ear to be tagged is held tightly by one hand while the pliers apply the tag with the other hand. Application seems virtually painless, very young calves barely flinch and make no protest whatever. Older calves most certainly *do* protest but this I believe is more from outraged feelings than from physical hurt. Calves are weighed and note taken of sex, weight, approximate age (i.e. in hours or days), area, and date of capture, which is set against the number of the tag used.

I found the best way when seeking calves was to get out really early, for I had six miles *to walk* before I got to the remote calving areas. This entailed a 3.30–4.00 a.m. start in the long daylight hours of June. Hinds which had calved the previous night, while in the corries for the night's grazing, were anxious to get to higher ground again, where they would spend the day, away from disturbance, heat and tormenting flies. Because of their young calves they often lagged behind the main body of deer to go out. One therefore looked for single hinds with a small calf following and then watched *unceasingly* until the calf, leg-weary in its extreme youth, lay down, when the hind, after lingering a little, would resume her progress to the higher ground. If one took one's eye off the hind and calf, even for seconds it seemed, the calf was sure to 'drop' in this time and could then prove difficult to find. Calves spotted by this method were often only hours old, and with their whereabouts pinpointed *painstakingly* before one set off over the distance which intervened, were usually relatively easy to secure. Calves, however, spotted by watching hinds returning to them in evening would naturally be older by twelve hours, often more perhaps, born in the preceding night and having the intervening day to add to this. They often proved difficult or impossible to catch, being strong enough to keep after the mother when she ran on the attempt being made to catch the calf. A hind with a strong calf would also often come back and encourage the calf on, where otherwise it might have 'dropped'. Meanwhile, the human pursuer, with bursting lungs, lags farther and farther behind and at last gives up, with the bitterness of several hours of watching now rendered abortive.

Average weights of calves of less than a day old was fourteen to fifteen pounds, with stags usually weighing heavier than hind calves. The lightest *live* calf weighed was a small hind calf of only ten pounds and the heaviest, also a hind calf, was one of twenty-six and a half pounds, rescued from a peat hole in which it had been trapped. On most days about eighteen to twenty miles were tramped, sometimes much more. My longest day in this time-consuming pursuit, was from 6.30 a.m. until 11.30 p.m., for two calves. About two-thirds of the calves tagged in each year were found between 5th and 17th June inclusive, after which numbers tailed off. Sexes evened out remarkably well in most seasons. In 1966 I tagged four stags all in one day and thought that therefore I'd have a preponderance of stags in that season. Next day, however, I tagged four hind calves. Totals over

61

the four seasons were sixty-eight hind calves and sixty-two stag calves.

In 1965, twenty-three calves were tagged, for twelve days out, and two dead calves were found. Hind calves thirteen; stag calves ten.

In 1966, thirty-five calves were tagged, for twenty days out, and two dead calves were found. Hind calves eighteen, stag calves seventeen.

In 1967 thirty-two calves were tagged for fourteen days out and one dead calf was found; sixteen of each sex.

In 1968 forty calves were tagged for fifteen days out and one dead calf found. Hind calves twenty-one; stag calves, nineteen.

During four seasons spent ear-tagging calves I learned much of deer behaviour. Some highlights of my calving seasons I give from my notes, freshly written each night while the day's events were still vivid.

I noted many cases where hinds brusquely repulsed calves which were not their own. This was a common occurrence, demonstrating their complete lack of tenderness for any calf not theirs. June 8th, '65. 'Spied at a lone hind with "black breeches" of peat, which was approaching a small green. A second hind also began to draw towards the green. As I watched, a small calf rose near the first hind and ran to her, only to be rudely, indeed, savagely repulsed, being knocked flat by a flailing foreleg. The second hind then went up to it and began nuzzling at it, whereupon it rose and began to suck. A clear case of mistaken identity on the part of the hapless calf.'

And on 6th June 1968: 'I saw a small calf with its mother. As I watched a nearby hind trotted over, nose outstretched inquiringly at the calf and then, as the calf in turn came towards her, she suddenly lashed out and knocked it flat.'

Again on 12th June 1967: 'Watched a hind with a large calf come down into the hags and saw another large calf approach her. The hind repulsed it in the usual savage manner, knocking it flat, but it got up and again approached, to be knocked over again.' There were times when I trembled for the spine of a soft-boned young calf, savagely floored by a hard hoof.

Of eagles, 7th June '65: 'Watched a hind bellowing mournfully and then begin to nose at what I then saw, through my glass, to be a dead calf. No obvious sign of injury but on skinning I found it had been killed by an eagle, with talon punctures on head and back, and lower jaws fractured. The mother must have arrived back in time to

62

repulse the eagle but too late to save her calf, which was a hind calf, fifteen pounds weight, less than a day old.'

And on 8th June: 'Saw a pair of eagles gliding high above the ridge and, later, over the calving coire. Looking for calves?'

12th June '67: 'I heard a "cheeping" note from somewhere ahead and, puzzled by it, I was thinking in terms of young grouse when I saw an eagle gliding around over the peat hags, an absurd sound for so huge a bird.'

18th June '68: 'Saw a hind on a green face stare fixedly at an object on the green which at first I suspected might be a calf. She then advanced on it, head and long neck outstretched, in interrogation as it were. The "object" took wing: an eagle, which flew to a vantage point above some hags, and sat there motionless for an hour.'

Of a successful day on 14th June '65: 'At 9.10 a.m. I spotted a hind begin calving. She didn't give birth till 11.17, with, beside her, a small group of cud-chewing hinds who paid no heed whatever to her. Lying down just prior to birth but suddenly sprang to her feet and simultaneously the calf *dropped* from her. She began cleaning it at once and within ten minutes it was on its feet, but kept collapsing on uncontrollable legs. It was nearly half an hour before it was success-ful in sucking—a six-minute feed being taken. Later, watched it *chew* peat from a nearby bank as also I observed an older calf do on 27th June '66. In the stomach of the eagle-killed calf there was a golf-ball-sized lump of peat so that it appears that deer calves *eat* a certain amount of peat to satisfy some need or other.'

At 2.10 p.m. on the same day: 'Saw a disturbed hind *galloping* down a hill face ahead of me with apparently the full length of her calf's two black-looking legs, with white-edged hooves, protruding from her and *waving wildly* about. She halted in the midst of a group of grazing hinds, in among deep hags, where she gave birth at 2.40, to a hind calf of fifteen and a half pounds, perfectly healthy despite its pre-natal careering.' This calf I saw in February 1969 as a healthy 3-year-old hind.

Of a successful evening capture on 17th June '65: 'Watched a single hind grazing for an hour and a half. At 4.30 p.m., her feeding abandoned, she set off eagerly downhill, and some 400 yards from where she'd been grazing her calf suddenly appeared and ran to meet her. Managed to get quite close before being seen. The calf, however, ran strongly behind her for half a mile before dropping, first running off slightly at a tangent. I then stalked it and popped the 'catcher' over its head. A large hind calf of nineteen pounds, and her loud squeals brought Ma and two other hinds to within fifty yards of me.'

Of an unsuccessful attempt at an evening capture, on 13th June '67: 'A hind at about 8.0 p.m. picked up her calf at the head of the burn but even though I got to within thirty yards before being seen the calf did not drop but followed the mother strongly, amazingly fleet for so tiny a calf, until they went out of sight.'

An example of searching an area for calves, late in the season, after a herd had moved out, occurred on 31st June '65:

'Out at 4 a.m. The tip of a crescent moon began to peep over the high ridge opposite my window, reminding me of the horns adorning a Viking's helmet, as I awoke at 3.30 a.m. Two hours later I watched a herd of sixty or so hinds move out from an area of rushes and greens. Searched this and found no less than seven calves; three ran before I got within distance of them at all, one 'near miss' which I really should have caught and three captures, all within twenty minutes. As the last of these calves ran I caught sight of another runner, about eight hundred yards away, a fox, which had not seen me. It appeared to be a dog fox for twice it lifted a hind leg and "anointed" tussocks as I watched. I had a very good view of it through my glass, in fact, it actually sat down on a ridge and watched the running deer calf intently but made no move to cut it off or molest it, as it presumably could have done. Obviously not hungry. I saw it set off, after the calf was out of sight, and make its way in the opposite direction, to a dead hind I had looked at half an hour before. It began sniffing around it in, at first, a care-free manner, only to be galvanized into speedy flight when it got my lingering scent.'

Of being almost trodden on by a hind eager to go to her calf on 29th June '66: 'As I watched, lying prone in the heather, I heard a hind's lowing call from out of the concealing mist. A moment or two later and a hind came out of the mist, heading straight for me. A very bleached-looking hind with eagerness incarnate in her every movement. She just could not contain her eager hurry and came pacing quickly past me, *not 5 feet* away so that I buried my betraying face in the heather. It was inevitable now that she would "wind" me and of course she ran, without disclosing her calf. That finished that, but it had been revealing to see the absolute eagerness of that hind.'

And on 5th July '66, another hind with a concealed calf: 'I saw a single hind below me, feeding. I lay down to watch her and shortly afterwards she too lay down, and began cudding, for two hours.

64

A two-year-old stag, ear-tagged as a day-old calf, for the purposes of research into the movements, longevity and general habits of red deer.

XXV

Calves are weighed and note is taken of their age and sex.

XXVI

The author holding a calf prior to tagging it while spying at another likely hind.

My two sons, Lea (fourteen) and Michael (eleven), always keen to assist in hill matters, helping in the ear-tagging of a red deer calf.

XXVII

XXVIII 'The calf did not drop, but followed the mother strongly.'

'Flash was almost on top of the deer calf before he owned to the scent.'

A recently born deer calf, still slimy-looking, with big sail-like ears.

XXIX

The hind which refused to go away fondling her new-born calf.

In winter roe deer eat a lot of ivy, and in doing so will rear up on
XXX their hind legs to reach tempting pieces.

Mature roe doe showing her very handsome throat patches.

Mature buck, in early March, antlers in velvet and good throat patches.

XXXII   Roe buck running his doe around in the ritual rutting ring from mid July to mid August; during this 'running' he will mate with her at intervals.

When she rose she grazed back and fore below me, within thirty yards at times for a further half-hour. She appeared greatly alarmed at one moment by four common gulls which flew back and fore, close above her head; she poked her head straight up and in the air, watching them, following their movements and looking as if she would bolt at any moment, her eye rolling in her head. It seems there must be an instinctive fear (of the eagle?) in having any largish bird above them; I have noted geese frighten deer into stampeding in more than one stalking season.

'Finally, the hind ceased grazing and made the characteristic bee-line to a spot only sixty yards from me, giving a very soft, muted lowing call, twice, barely audible. The concealed calf, which had been out of my immediate view, below a rocky outcrop, ran up to meet her at this, and began eagerly to feed, small tail wagging ecstatically. When it had finished I got up, hoping it would drop when the hind ran, but it too ran. I raced after them and, while out of my sight the calf dropped, but the hind gave the game away by returning to look at me, "barking" at me twice. I searched and found the calf, but, before I got near, it got up and ran again and I gave it up.'

There is a belief that very young calves lying motionless give off very little body scent, and this would seem borne out by an experience on 31st May '66. 'Saw a lone hind run from an area of hags below me. Leaving the pointer, Flash, which I had out with me, leashed to my stick, I searched the area, and found first the glaringly obvious "afterbirth" and, only yards away, the new-born calf. After tagging it I took Flash down to see if he would own to its scent, but no, he was almost *on top of it* before he did so, and froze.'

Regarding the 'afterbirth', hinds always eat this with every appearance of avidity. A theory which has been put forward is that this is partly to be rid of its betraying appearance and strong scent, which might draw avian or four-legged predators to the area of the calf.

Of ptarmigan chicks on 8th June '66: 'As I neared the military road I suddenly heard an alarmed "cheep-cheep" behind me, and turning caught a glimpse of a yellow ball of fluff legging it off while simultaneously a hen ptarmigan almost brushed my shoes as she did the age-old decoy act, grovelling almost flat before me, white wings outstretched and trailing. Whereas the cock at this time is a mottled grey, she was a mottled golden-brown which blended with the high-ground mosses to perfection. Satisfied that she had drawn my eyes

65

from her chick's retreat, she too withdrew, and although I searched not a chick could I find.'

And again on 15th June '66: 'I came on another ptarmigan brood with an even bolder hen. I managed to catch a chick, to photograph, and she came, a bustling, bristling, feathered fury, and half a dozen times rose, at short range, and flew straight up at my face. Her mate lent only moral support, keeping his distance.'

On 9th June '66 a decamping calf actually came back towards me before lying down: 'Followed the departing hind and calf up the steep face just as fast as my protesting legs allowed. At the top saw a group of hinds moving off and a single hind lingering behind, looking back with that characteristic worried, maternal look. Just about to go forward and search when a calf's head popped over a rise only yards away, *coming towards me*. Spotting me, it *dropped at once*. On a very bare place so I left it for a moment or so. Obviously, it felt very bare too and almost immediately rose and, crossing to a peat bank, lay down in its cover. Retreated, crept in above the bank and popped my "catcher" over its head just as it turned to bolt.'

On this day, also: 'Just ahead of me I saw a group of hinds collected around a peat hag, where a single hind was standing. The group, feminine curiosity paramount, were approaching in turn, heads and necks outstretched, sniffing. I at once suspected a calf but then wondered if it were not simply "wallow" behaviour. The single hind, who seemed the cynosure of her curious sisters, then lay down and stretching head and neck, bellowed in smug satisfaction. I went forward at once, the hinds ran and there was the calf, struggling to stand up, very recently born, on the black moistiness of the hag.'

Of another calf, conspicuous also in its background, on 10th June '66: 'Followed without much hope, a hind and her small calf, which went out of sight. Found the calf only because it elected to drop on a bare green, instead of in nearby heather and peat hags.'

Of a hind which almost trampled on me on hearing her calf squeal, on 13th June '66: 'The calf squealed lustily, in outrage, and brought the mother charging down the soft green banks so fast that she dug deep into the soft green, leaving skid-marks when she braked on seeing me. She had the squeal absolutely pinpointed and had I been a predator she was obviously out for blood.'

Of two calves lying very near each other, on 15th June '66. 'Saw a hind, one of a disturbed herd, lingering and looking back. Spying in

66

the direction at which she was "pointing" I found a calf lying curled up. As I came to it, to my great surprise, there was the "bonus" of another calf lying within ten yards of it. Secured both though the second tried a bolt at last minute. A stag calf and exceedingly vociferous which brought a dozen hinds, in from above and below, to investigate. On release it ran at once and I watched the mother run across to it, sniff at it and lead it away. The other calf lay still and did not squeal, nor bolt for it, a younger calf.'

Of an occasion when a hind 'overshot' where her calf was lying, on 17th June '66; 'A lone hind feeding, in evening, drew my gaze. She grazed for about ten minutes, pausing at intervals for a scrutiny all around her. And then as a sharp, stinging rain-shower began she literally bolted downhill so that I, too, had to run like mad to keep her in view. She "overshot" her calf for I saw her halt and retrace her steps, then begin licking a calf which came to meet her. Without letting it suck she began to move down into the coire and so I gambled all on a rush for her. She ran, the calf dropped and I got it easily.'

It became apparent in that year that up to two to three days after birth calves do not move far. Recoveries made and marked calves which were re-sighted seemed to show this quite definitely.

On 21st June '66 I had the experience of having a very young calf, uncharacteristically, follow the hind instead of dropping: 'When I saw it struggling to get to its feet I realized I had just missed its birth by minutes. Gave it time to get stronger and watched for an hour, during which time the mother lay on and though the calf, getting visibly stronger on its legs, nuzzled her recumbent form pleadingly, she did not rise to let it suck. When the calf lay down I made an approach but over the very bare ground was still three hundred yards distant when the hind made off uphill. *Incredibly* the hour-old calf followed, the hind stopping to wait twice, encouraging it on. They disappeared over a ridge and I was sure I would lose the calf in the broken ground above but as I, at last, topped the ridge gasping for breath, I saw the hind ahead, the calf still valiantly following but now obviously flagging. Caught it without much difficulty and though it squealed as I did so, drawing in half a dozen apprehensive mothers, it quietened and lay quite still as I left it.'

Tried the experiment of 'squealing' myself on 22nd June '66, with success. 'Drew a hind to within fifty yards by "calf-squealing" at her, while all the time I stood in full view.'

Of another 'squealer' on 27th June '66: 'A golden plover was calling plaintively beyond the burn and this brought a hind running in anxiously to the burn banks, where she "picked up" a very small calf, hitherto unsuspected, but which I later caught and ear-tagged, with due gratitude to the golden plover.'

Calving began, in 1967, on 5th June, much the same as in 1966. 'Sat down to spy the coire and spotted two single hinds low on its banks. Then below and to the west of them I saw a single hind standing and with her a very tottery-legged calf, having its first suck. She went just out of sight behind a hillock, the calf tottering behind her, and I made for them then. As I did so one of the recumbent hinds arose and began "bellowing". At first I thought she was bellowing while en route to her calf but then the rather "distraught" note of her bellowing struck me forcibly and I wondered if she was mourning a dead calf. Cautiously approaching the hillock which hid the hind and calf I got my camera ready. I crept the last few yards and found the hind, head up and ears wide-spread, looking straight at me. Kept very still and though she kept bobbing her head about, for some minutes, in an attempt to identify the strange object, she was eventually reassured. Her calf was tottering about on widespread spindly legs near her, unable to make up its mind whether to lie down or to go to mother. The hind grazed a little, and then bellowed, adopting a posture like a stag roaring, except that her tongue lolled out of one side of her mouth. She bellowed, in seeming complacency and pleased self-satisfaction, more than once as I watched and photographed her. The calf wandered over on legs still unsteady and she sniffed at it, licking it in a caressing manner. A fine looking hind with silver-grey eyes, as had her calf, instead of the normal deep-brown eyes.

'After successfully catching and tagging the calf, on my way up the coire, I almost stepped on a hen grouse which rose off nine eggs. Crossing one of the green gullies which "cut up" this coire I found a recently dead calf apparently still-born. It seemed I had been correct in my interpretation of the "bellowing" of the other hind, as if in mourning.'

Of a calf which lay down in a pool of water, 7th June 1967: 'A hind calf of about twelve hours old. It made off on release and actually chose to lie down in a peaty pool of about three inches in depth.'

On 7th June also: 'Watched a hind arrive at my "scent" where I'd

68

slid down the hill-face, stalking a calf. She shied back violently, retreated a few steps, looked as if she was going to bolt, but then, hesitantly, plucking up courage, quickly crossed my trail. Obviously, going to her calf.'

Of an occasion when a weak 'last year's calf', i.e. a yearling, was chivvied away from a herd by a mature hind: 'While I was watching a small herd about 6.30 a.m. I saw a very weak yearling being driven away by a dark-coated hind. Actually chased the obviously ailing yearling (which is probably marked for death) away and at one point kicked her legs in the air and rose up on her hindlegs, striking out with her forelegs while the yearling jumped hastily into a deep hag to dodge her. The yearling made no attempt to rejoin the herd, but wandered off very dispiritedly towards the burn banks, unwanted and unwell, a hard, unfeeling existence.'

On 12th June 1967 an experience with a 'lazy' calf: 'As I came to a ridge I glimpsed a hind and saw she had a calf. Made a rush but the calf followed strongly and the hind was one of those who wait and encourage their calves to follow. I kept running and gained a little and the calf, though still running strongly, suddenly jumped aside and lay down. The hind actually came back as if to say, "Come on, you're old enough to run," but it lay on and I secured it easily. Bigger than I'd realized, a stag calf of twenty and a half pounds.'

A calf which 'adopted' me on 13th June 1967: 'Though it had squealed and struggled at first, it began to follow me after I'd tagged it, and I had some trouble losing it.'

On the same day I stalked a very wide-awake looking calf *in my stocking soles* to avoid its hearing my approach, and got it.

A 'cavalry charge' by ten hinds on 19th June '67: 'Saw a hind come back into the coire from a herd I'd disturbed. A "calf squeal" from me took her in fast but had also the unlooked for effect of bringing ten others charging down the steep coire like a troop of cavalry. It being obvious that there were calves about I searched and ultimately secured three.'

A very rewarding day was 26th June 1967, when I saved the life of a deer calf. 'I lay and spied at a single hind whose behaviour began increasingly to intrigue me. She kept returning to one particular green "runner" (i.e. a strip of green which often covers an underground stream) and there she would bellow mournfully. I could spy no calf and the hind wandered off eventually, though with reluctance, out of my view. I marked down the place well and made for it later,

69

expecting to find a dead calf. Instead, I found a roughly circular hole in the peat, no more than nine inches across and to its edge an obvious track, worn by the hind. I poked my stick into it and, about four feet down, I touched soft peat. I stirred it around in what was obviously an underground cavity and was electrified by the high-pitched squeal of a calf. But how had it got in, and how was I to get it out? The cavern below was in Stygian gloom and I could see no sign of the squealer nor could I enlarge the hole. I explored a little way up the runner and then came upon a slightly larger hole down which I might *just* squeeze. I had first to divest myself of jacket and jersey in order to squeeze through and inside, in semi-darkness I descried a tunnel in the soft peat through which I could *just* wriggle at the expense of a liberal coating of mucky wet peat. This was pot-holing with a vengeance and I did not relish it one little bit; would I perhaps get stuck underground, miles from anywhere, with no aid possible? Needs must, however, if I was to save the immured calf and so I squeezed myself through, hearing as I did so the calf moving at its end of the constricting tunnel. Reaching forward as I neared the end of it I was able to grasp the hindlegs of the now vigorously protesting calf and sliding, literally, backwards in the wet, peaty tunnel I drew it out after me like a cork out of a bottle until I could rise at the larger hole and emerge out of the depths. I almost laughed in amusement and relief at the sight of the peat-black calf and at my own appearance, likewise black. The calf, a big hind calf at least ten days old, weighed twenty-six and a half pounds. It had obviously "dropped in" at the larger hole and unable to jump out had squeezed through the tunnel in an attempt to get out, but had neither sense nor courage to squeeze back, while the mother probably kept "encouraging" it at the smaller hole through which she could smell and hear her. The calf was four feet underground and had it not been for the mother's persistence in returning to the hole and my fortuitous sighting of her, she would have died there.' As it was, she survived. I saw her the following year, still with her ear-tag firmly on. My wife's remarks when she saw the state of my clothes that night I will not record.

A glimpse of a hind 'guarding' her concealed calf was vouchsafed me on 10th June 1968: 'The coire was a bowl of mist. Glimpsed a hind there in a temporary clearing of the mist and sat down to wait. A grouse near me began that aggravating "cack-cack" of unconfirmed suspicion and I rose at last to try and "shoo" it off before it alarmed my hind. As might have been expected the mist too rose at that precise moment and the hind got a fleeting glimpse before I froze again. She had undoubtedly been hearing the grouse and she now became a perfect study of undecided suspicions pulling her one way and maternal feelings pulling her the other. At one point she started right away and got well up the coire before she stopped, tarried a little, then drawn by a force greater than apprehension, came slowly back. Visibility was now good and when a few deer came grazing slowly up the coire the hind went to meet them and "convoyed" them past where she, obviously, had her calf hidden. At one point she faced up to the last hind with a vixenish expression, as if ready to rear up and lash out at her. Later a few sheep renewed her apprehensions and these too she watched past but not so closely as she had the deer. She was the perfect picture of a hind with a calf lying nearby, absolutely unmistakable. Up and down she paced for an hour while I tried to shrink deeper into the heather as the sun grew brighter. I amused myself by trying to guess the whereabouts of the calf but in the event was 200 yards out, a considerable distance in the rough ground. I must have watched for two and a half hours before she eventually went to it and I then secured it easily, a small calf twelve hours of age.'

The unrest caused by heat and midges was apparent on 12th June: 'The hind fed on a little, then lay down about 50 yards from her calf, but was quite unable to rest because of the midges. Three times she shifted position, but at last, as if something had snapped, she got up and *raced* down to some deeper peat hags, whose moistness might give her some relief.'

On 15th June, of a very young calf: 'Very recently born, black, ugly and slimy looking with big sail-like ears looking out of all proportion to its head. And yet a scant twelve hours later and it would be a picture of red-brown, dappled charm with well-proportioned ears. It *crawled* to meet me at first, then rose on very shaky legs and staggered forward. I'm sure it would, at this stage, have greeted the appearance of a fox in similar fashion. It attempted to suck the very unrewarding lower edge of my jacket.'

An example of how the instinct to lie still in an attempt to evade detection is still latent in red deer, even on the bare hill, I saw one day in early June '69: 'My eye was caught by a light-coloured "lump" like a hummock of bleached grass, lying opposite and quite close to me as I came out of the burn banks. Curious, I spied at it. It

71

was a hind, bleached in her old winter hair, lying with her head and neck outstretched along the ground, like any young calf, and beside her the dappled form of her new calf. She had obviously seen me as I came out of the burn and elected to lie still instead of giving the game away by running. She had almost succeeded in her ruse but seeing by my approach that she was discovered, she rose and ran, leaving the calf lying.'

The most remarkable maternal feeling I have ever known in a hind occurred on 18th June 1968: 'Out at 6 a.m. spied a hind low in a coire who seemed near to calving, at 8.30 a.m. She lay down in some long rushes but, in obvious discomfort, was soon up again and standing straddle-legged. Twice she bellowed and she was obviously straining as she stood. By 9.45 she had a foot of black legs showing and the "water-bag" was dangling low between her back legs. She lay down at 9.50 and was up again almost at once, at 10.10. Lay down at 10.15 and at 10.20 the calf was born. She did not bellow at all after the birth but was "lowing" to her calf a lot. I stalked her then from my vantage point about three-quarters of a mile distant, and got within twenty yards, though at one stage she grew suspicious, giving one or two half-hearted barks and leaving her calf momentarily. I froze for what seemed an interminable period and she eventually relaxed with her calf again.

'I took some photos, though the long rushes hid the calf most of the time. It was very tottery-legged and often attempted to suck while between the *fore-legs* of the hind. I watched for four hours and the calf sucked, successfully, four times in that period. The "afterbirth" was still dangling from the hind until about an hour after the calf's birth, by which time she had eaten it all. Much of it she stripped from herself, her head poked under one upraised hind-leg as she pulled at it. The last bit fell away of its own accord and she ate this also, with apparent relish. She also drank thirstily at intervals. I used up all my film, eventually *sitting up*, *in full view at 20 yards* and the hind saw me, *but took no notice*. Even when I stood up, she did not run but stayed where she was now lying, with her calf. I expected her to run when I approached to tag the calf but she only rose and stood over it, twisting her mouth in a grimace of apprehension at me, grating her teeth audibly. I was within six feet of her before she retreated a little, but then *back she came* still twisting her mouth and grating her teeth, now the very picture of nervous alarm, nostrils flaring, eyes rolling and her teeth grinding as she worked her jaws,

72

yet run she would not. I had eventually, to "shoo" her away, the only wild red deer I have ever encountered which stood its ground in the face of a dreaded human. I tagged the calf quickly and left, having no doubt that so dauntless a mother would soon be back to a reunion with the calf she had so valiantly conquered her own fears to protect.'

7

Roe, Sika and Other Small 'Deer'

THE period March to May is probably the best of the year for seeing roe, and indeed, this holds good for Japanese Sika also. With the trees still leafless and bracken and other undergrowth at a minimum, the small and dainty roe deer, with their penchant for cover, so elusive in the months of lush summer foliage and undergrowth, became much more visible.

Roe deer in their winter coat, thicker and darker than the thin foxy-red of summer, have very attractive throat patches or gorgets, which to me add distinction to their already abundant charm. Not all roe have the same patches so that these greyish-white markings can aid in identifying individuals, particularly does who lack antlers as an aid to identity. The most common pattern, very well marked in mature roe, is an upper transverse band girdling the front of the throat just below the 'chin' and below this an almost geometrically square patch. A variation of this is in having the upper band split, so as to be in two halves, more or less each side of the windpipe, while the lower patch may be crescent-shaped. In others the upper or lower patch may be missing, leaving only a single patch, while a very few may have no gorgets whatever. These very attractive gorgets follow the same pattern, on individual roe, year after year, a very handy guide to individuals where roe are plentiful.

Roe, as their woodland habitat would suggest, eat a lot of 'browse' in their daily feeding. A most charming sight I witnessed, on a day in early May, was of a buck and a doe, daintily browsing, shoulder deep

75

at times with only their heads visible, on the golden-yellow flowers of a patch of prickly whins (gorse). I watched, entranced, for fifteen minutes and in all that time they never once ceased, nipping off flower after flower, avidly, yet with that daintiness implicit in all roe movements. On ivy too they will browse eagerly, rising erect on their hind legs to reach its tempting greenness.

I make no secret of the fact that I regard roe as the most delightful of animals and roe fawns the most attractive of all youngsters. In the Highlands fawns are usually born in late May or in June. Unlike red deer calves, born on the treeless hill, roe fawns are born in the cover of woodlands. This makes their discovery all the harder and perhaps that is why the memories of these scant findings linger the longer: of twins, only a day or so old, lying, curled up together, above a brawling river, among fronds of bracken; of the shrill, piercing shriek which once almost petrified me when a tiny, dappled fawn burst from bracken at my feet, emitting that ear-piercing, panic-stricken cry incredible in its intensity from one so tiny, before running fast away, and vanishing anew in the bracken; or of the courageous doe who circled me closely one June as I knelt to photograph her fawn. From a friend I learnt of how another courageous doe, fiercely maternal, had chased his terrier off, striking at it with sharp front hooves, undoubtedly the way she would have treated a hunting fox. Roe fawns, however, do turn up fairly regularly at fox dens; they weigh only about four and a half pounds at birth and present no difficulty, in killing or carrying, to a hungry fox, in the absence of the protecting presence of the doe.

One of the most delightful glimpses to be seen is that of a doe returning to her fawn after some hours' absence. The fawn lies hidden as she approaches until the doe emits an almost inaudible wheezy exhalation of breath, a faint 'wheee', which brings the youngster to its feet and bounding to meet her. A fawn, or fawns, will usually be suckled standing, but when very young may be suckled while both mother and young are lying. This I have never seen with red deer but red deer calves seem to get the use of their legs more quickly than roe fawns, for a recently born roe fawn will collapse like a house of cards, its legs folding uncontrollably under it, if one attempts to put it on its legs.

Attractive and dainty as roe look, the buck can be savagery incarnate in the annual territory or rutting fights. I am convinced that there are more casualties as a result of these than in the much larger red deer. In the territory fights, in which the older bucks chase out the younger ones (often their own offspring) from the area which they regard as theirs, usually in May, little damage may be done, for usually the odds are weighted in that a much stronger buck is chasing out a younger buck who knows better than to try and argue.

I witnessed such a chase one evening when not more than a hundred yards from my house I was almost knocked over by two madly racing bucks, one just behind the other. Nor was this play; an air of deadly menace was implicit in the pursuit as they ran at full stretch with no time for the graceful arching bounds so often seen when one disturbs roe. As they almost met me, the leading buck dodged swiftly and ran back the way they'd come. His pursuer overshot me and raced on past into some birches above me where he halted and 'barked' repeatedly, staccato, savage-sounding barks as of violence thwarted by my appearance. Returning home after my short evening walk I saw the other buck, about two hundred yards below where I'd first encountered them, standing spent-looking and silent. Not for him the self-advertising savagery of the stronger buck, but a prudent self-effacing silence.

Nor is the buck notably tender towards his doe at the rut. I noted on 29th July one year: 'The buck was running the doe around for about 15 minutes at a time, then both lay up for at least half an hour, looking absolutely spent. The pattern of their mating was for the buck to run the doe round in a roughly oval course for some time, during which she would halt at intervals. The buck would then cover her (he did this 4 times at one "running"' period) or he might actually "fork" her on with a by no means gentle prod of his antlers in her haunch. A rest period ensued and then the pattern was repeated.'

Japanese Sika deer, introduced to Loch Ness side about 1900, perhaps make even more use of natural cover, and are even more adept at lying tight when they think they are undetected, than are roe deer. These deer have adapted themselves superlatively well and from a mere half dozen or so there are now, all along the south-east side of Loch Ness, probably upwards of three hundred or so. This must be one of the biggest concentrations of Sika deer in Scotland, though there are also Sika deer in Ross-shire, and in Kintyre there is a concentration which may be even higher than on Loch Ness side. In size Japanese Sika fall roughly between roe and red deer, with antlers very similar to those of red deer but seldom bearing more than eight points. These antlers are usually narrow of span and rather upright, lacking the curve and sweep of a good red stag's antlers. They are often light-coloured and the points may be short and blunt. In build the Sika is stockier and more thickset than red or roe; a mature stag in particular gives one the impression of a pocket Hercules, of compact and potentially explosive power. As it 'bounces' away, with the very typical 'rocking-chair' gait, one gets the impression of a very flat-looking broad back and well-filled, plump haunches, often accentuated by the white rump-patch, flared out or expanded in alarm. This gait is very distinct from that of red or roe: Sika seem to bounce away on stiffly-held legs, vanishing quickly for all that.

For most of the year Sika deer have a thick-looking coat of very dark looking brown, in fact in winter it appears jet-black, with a very prominent white rump which can be expanded at will in moments of alarm. The tail is longer than that of red deer. In the short summer months, however, Sikas have coats so different as to make one incredulous that they are the same species. Probably the most handsome summer coat of all our deer, it is then a deep, rich red, most handsomely marked with lines of creamy dapples while the rump patch looks heart-shaped, smaller and yellower than in winter, distinctively outlined by a broad, dark band. Seen against the pale, fresh green of early July bracken, in sunlight, the Sika stag makes a picture long remembered.

Their calving, mating seasons, and, in the stag, antler casting and re-growth are similar to those of red deer, whereas their habitat is that of roe, the birch and hazel woods which fringe river and loch. It would seem that they compete with roe to some extent for this habitat, for when Sika numbers rise to any extent so do roe appear to decline or, indeed, vanish. To a certain extent, also, Sikas overlap with red deer, for one may see Sikas on the bare hill, though never far from the tree-line, and one will get red deer in the woods on occasions. There is in fact certain evidence of cross-breeding between the species, probably between a Jap stag and a red hind, but this, though authenticated, is rare. The Sika stag has a rutting cry which is for all the world like a very loud whistle, tailing off into a weird scream, usually thrice repeated. Very eerie, indeed, can this sound, in wild country at dawn or dusk, when it is most frequently heard. There is a certain ventriloquial element in this 'whistle' which makes it hard to pinpoint, much harder than that of a rutting red stag, for instance. The rut seems very prolonged, for I have heard 'whistles' from early

78

September to early January. The alarm call of Sika is also a 'whistle' but just one short, sharply-exhaled, squealing whistle, much less in intensity than the thrice-repeated rutting 'whistle'. These 'whistles' of Sika are so utterly unlike what one expects to hear from deer that it is often difficult to convince anyone hearing it for the first time that it was, indeed, deer which uttered it.

Of their lying tight proclivities I have had ample evidence. My first instance of this was when coming home from a day at grouse, in late August, we saw on the hill fringe of a scattered birch wood a richly dappled Sika stag, lying apparently asleep on a bare green. We walked straight to him, and he lay motionless until we had almost stepped on him, when he rose and made off in one spring-heeled bound. Another such instance I gave in a previous book, *Highland Year*, when I did everything but 'kick up' a Sika stag lying doggo in a *small* patch of heather. I have walked towards bracken, on Loch Ness side, with a strong wind bearing my scent ahead, and yet Sika have jumped out of it only when I had almost stumbled over them. In the summer woodlands in fact a quest in search of Sika during most of the daylight hours can be even more unrewarding than a search for roe deer. There will be plenty about but they will lie tight in cover, from which they will only become active as evening arrives, seeking cover again shortly after dawn. They are even fonder of 'wallowing' in peat than are red deer, and unlike red deer often use 'dry' peat banks to rub on as well as the semi-liquid rolling pools. I am convinced, in fact, that the first darkening of the summer's dappled coat is induced 'artificially', on the part of the stags at least, by this habit, which is indulged in by the stags as soon as they clean the velvet from their antlers in early autumn and continues throughout their 'rut'. The true black-looking, thick winter coat grows in under cover of this premature darkening. The Sikas are at any rate interesting and very decorative additions to our cervidae, even though they are not indigenous.

The wild goats which occur here and there throughout the Highlands are perhaps best distinguished as being the only animal which man, even with his very inefficient civilized nose, could track by scent. In stalking these goats, as wild as the very deer and much sharper in the eye, I have been able to follow their track through long heather rankly redolent of goat. There was at one time a herd of these on a high, rocky hill at the Fort Augustus end of Loch Ness, but there are none there now. One of the last of these, a very fine 'billy', apparently swam Loch Ness, perhaps in search of female company and appeared in a forestry plantation on its north side. The forester there saw him on one occasion and coveted his hirsute coat for a rug, not being aware that 'stench' and wild goat are inseparable. He instructed the stalker to shoot and skin the goat for him. In due course the stalker did so but unable to stomach the smell, so far from skinning it he avowed, on later inquiry from the forester, that the goat had 'vanished', as indeed he had.

Blue or mountain hares have likewise almost vanished from the hills above Fort Augustus though in the 1920s they were so numerous that, in the graphic words of Johnny Kytra, 'there was a hare beside every stone'. He told me of hare drives in those days when the panniers of the ponies would be filled to bursting and a sackful of hares would be slung across the middle of them. About 1930 the blue hares vanished to the point where it is an occasion to see one nowadays. My most memorable experience with a blue hare occurred in June one year, out on the high ridge of Corrieyairack. So well camouflaged was the hare that I was almost on top of it before I saw it, crouched motionless below a grey, lichen-adorned rock. Aware by my sudden stop and scrutiny that it had been detected the hare made off with its clumsy-looking lope, but stopped near the top of the ridge, and so I screwed my telephoto lens onto my camera to try for a photograph. As I was doing so, seated in full view on the bare green and rock-scattered slope, the hare began, unbelievably, to lope leisurely down towards me. In increasing excitement and frustration I kept trying to focus on its approaching form, expecting to see it run off at a tangent at any moment but in vain; it kept moving 'out of focus'. I might have saved myself my dangerously mounting blood-pressure. The hare, leading me to consider coining a new phrase, 'As mad as a June hare', paid no heed to my crouching form but continued to approach, ending up by sitting again below the very slab it had vacated. And there I took photographs to my heart's content and had almost to force the sitter to go when I got up. A painstaking search revealed no young ones, the only *logical* solution that occurred to me for this particular hare's midsummer madness.

An animal which almost vanished as a species but which is now increasing again, possibly as a result of the increase in coniferous woods throughout the Highlands, is the pine marten. Even in the 1840s, when Charles St John was writing so attractively on Highland wild life, the pine marten was apparently regarded as relatively rare;

A roe doe with her day-old fawn, exhibiting strong
maternal attachment.

XXXIII

Roe twins, a day or so old, left lying in the cover of bracken while the doe is away feeding.

A day-old Japanese Sika calf, showing the domed skull and narrow 'snipey' muzzle which is typical of Sika deer.

A typical 'family' party of Sika deer in their dark winter coat: a hind, her yearling and her calf of that year.

XXXVI
A Japanese Sika stag in dark winter coat, showing the white rump and the grizzled facial markings.

A fine wild billy goat, locally fairly common in the north-west Highlands.

The blue or mountain hare, now rather scarce in the north-west Highlands, though still common in the dryer north-east Highlands.

The pine marten, an attractive animal, of vivacious and alert expression.

A wildcat, snarling its defiance from the crotch of an oak tree, after being 'treed' by the author's terriers.

XXXVIII

The wildcat is widespread, though not abundant throughout the Highlands. Average weight is 11–12 lb., but weights of up to 17 lb. have been recorded.

Otters are seldom seen very far from water, but the author has come upon them making journeys overland.

XXXIX

Stoats are not numerous in the Highlands. In winter they have a complete coat change to white except for the black tip to the tail.

In the Highlands, when sand is not available, badgers make their homes in the depths of rock cairns.

An adder, our only venomous snake but one which is never aggressive for aggression alone.

but judging from his encounters with the species it was more common than it is today. There has, however, been a very definite, if unspectacular, increase in Inverness-shire of late years and pine martens are now known to be in Glengarry and Glenmoriston and certainly as far down the Great Glen as the vicinity of Loch Lochy side, where an acquaintance of mine had a family of them reared in his rather unfrequented farm-loft in 1968.

Typically musteline in appearance but with a 'sweeter' expression than that of a stoat, the pine marten has a rich, dark, chocolate-brown, glossy coat with a very handsome frontlet (throat and chest) of, in some cases, deep orange, though it varies from orange-yellow to yellow-white. The pale-coloured insides and edges of the rounded ears are striking against the dark brown head, and the expression is that of vivacious alertness. The male is larger than the female, about thirty-three inches in length overall, against her thirty inches, and heavier, at four and a half pounds to her three pounds or so. The tail is almost squirrel-like in its bushiness, as befits an animal partly arboreal. From all accounts pine martens are catholic in their diet (St John records one raiding his raspberries), which includes birds' eggs, fledgelings, rats, mice, voles, rabbits, berries of all sorts and even carrion. I have been told that in North-west Scotland they have been suspected of robbing eagles' eyries, and at the other extreme, of scavenging roadside litterbins. There seems no doubt that they can be very bold on occasion. An acquaintance in the Invergarry area had one come regularly every night one winter to his bird table, illuminated, when once he became aware of this, by the light from a nearby window. Less admirable and indeed, less advisable for their own safety is their habit of raiding hen-houses, when usually *every* hen is killed in an orgy of blood lust. As they invariably return to eat at one of the carcasses they are usually trapped by a naturally vengeful poultry owner.

Twice in the last year or two pine martens have been found drowned between the lock gates on the Culachy stretch of the Caledonian Canal, unable to get out up the perpendicular stone-faced walls.

Otters are always with us but are seen very infrequently, perhaps just a round, sleek head, surfacing only momentarily on a backwater of the Canal, a string of bubbles the only clue as to where it has then gone, for of the otter itself there will be no further trace. I envy the sighting by a close friend of an otter on Mull repeatedly climbing up a huge, seaweed-grown rock, to slide down its sloping side in the slippery weed, with every appearance of enjoyment. My own clearest view of an otter was when it was out of its element, on land in fact, very early one June morning, walking ahead of me up the path I was using. The path was about fifty yards above the river Tarff, which here ran in a series of deep, narrow gorges with waterfalls pouring into and out of every black pool. Obviously, the otter preferred the easier going of the path than either the rough turbulence of the river or the bracken and fern-choked river banks. My first glimpse was of it hurriedly leaving the path and vanishing in the fern, and then of a luxuriantly-whiskered round, dark head poking out from the fern as its owner surveyed the early-morning interloper. Satisfied but apparently in no whit alarmed it made its leisurely way with lissom, sinuous, arching, ferret-like movement along the bank below where I walked, and twice actually came up to the path's edge, to retreat each time more, it seemed, in disgust than in fear, as I drew near. It vanished at last around a bend ahead and I saw it no more.

One does not associate the aquatic otter with overland journeys. Neither does one associate the wildcat with water, yet a most reliable friend was treated to the sight of one swimming with every appearance of expertise across the Caledonian Canal, on a quiet, lonely stretch. Nor had it been alarmed or pursued by anything; himself unseen, he watched it leisurely enter the canal and swim across to his side, where it shook itself vigorously before vanishing into the vegetation of the bankside.

I was myself incredibly lucky in being able to stalk and photograph a wildcat while driving through coniferous woodland some years back. My friend Barry spotted the cat first when driving along on a rather dull and drizzly evening as it crossed the rough road ahead of us. It then crossed a small burn below the road, and began to have a clean-up, apparently disliking the wet feet it had got in crossing the burn. By this time we had stopped and I had my 400 mm. telephoto lens screwed onto my camera. I took a snap but it was very far out and so, to derisive snorts from my two boys, also with us, I got very quietly out of the Land Rover, freezing whenever the assiduously licking cat looked up, continuing my stealthy approach only when it resumed cleaning. Inching forward, prone on the ground, freezing and progressing in turn, I got down to the burn and noiselessly across it, shielded by a small hillock. Noise was now the thing to be avoided; I was very near, but out of sight. At last I gained the hillock-top to see the cat still intent on its toilet, only thirty feet away. The light was so poor that I had to use a very slow shutter speed, and therefore had to have the cat absolutely still. I made a clicking sound with my tongue and the cat looked fair at me, another click, of shutter this time, and I had it on film.

So excited was I—a *wildcat* at thirty feet, in my camera viewfinder —that my hands were shaking, adding to the hazard of camera shake with a long-focus lens. The cat recommenced 'washing up' and I again halted it and photographed it. A third time and the wildcat, its reputation for ferocity deserved, I feel sure, only in self-defence rather than in aggression towards humans, decided that the place was really getting too noisy, and rising, sauntered off in a very leisurely way, vanishing into the dark conifers.

Badgers, those relatively inoffensive and almost entirely nocturnal animals, are very definitely on the increase in Inverness-shire now-a-days. Johnny Kytra, with a lifetime on Culachy, told me that until thirty years ago he had never encountered badgers on his rounds through the hill or at fox den time, when *all known* sandholes and cairns were visited. The situation is very different now, for many of these same holes and cairns are now occupied by badger to the exclusion of the fox. I have often read of the fox taking over a badger sett but here it has more often been the other way round, though on occasion a fox has reoccupied a sett where badgers have moved out. Badgers occur here now within a few hundred yards of the village, and at the other extreme out in a lonely glen where eagles and deer are their nearest neighbours. Out in such hill glens as this, where sandholes are scarce, badgers use cairns of rock as setts and I would defy any badger-digger to reach them in these. In such a cairn there is unfortunately little sign of whether the occupant is badger or fox, no huge ramp of sand mixed with old bedding material, as at a sand-hole sett, and often the only way is to let the terriers in, when in due course the typical shuddering snorting of an enraged badger gives a clue. It is in these encounters that the Highland stalker has cause for grievance with badgers for, even though only in defence of their homes, they can inflict deadly injury on terriers. I had wondered how these injuries could be caused by a badger until I saw, by lucky chance, a boar badger fighting off three terriers in a cairn. He came time after time up to the rocky threshold of his cairn, driving the dogs out with lightning slashes to right and left with his iron-muscled, long-clawed forefeet. After that demonstration, I no longer

83

wondered how a terrier could have hair, skin and flesh torn off its head and left dangling. However, though a very occasional badger may turn rogue and raid henhouses (and in this I have caught a badger, old and almost toothless, *in flagrante delicto*) they are relatively inoffensive and indeed attractive, with most glimpses being in car headlights as they cross roads at night unless one is a sett-watcher. A sow badger, a road casualty, I investigated once contained only earth-worms, literally scores of them, a tribute to the innocuousness of much of the badger's diet.

Stoats are not numerous around Culachy. Johnny Kytra has had one or two fascinating glimpses of them, due to his habit of sitting, contemplatively, on some handy rock, while he enjoyed a pipeful of strong tobacco. Once he watched a big stoat approach, carrying a young rabbit retriever fashion, in its jaws, 'with an air of pride'. Proud of its own strength it might well have been for the victim was bigger than the 'retriever'. On another occasion he watched a stoat come busily back and forth to a disused rabbit burrow. Nine times it passed, each time carrying a large vole. Whether the sandhole contained young stoats, or was just a cache for a 'rainy' day he did not know.

The only venomous snake on the British list, the adder, is not numerous either, though Glen Moriston was at one time regarded as having a lot of adders. From one who was brought up as a child in this glen I was told, 'We always had to be ready, when playing outdoors as children, to jump high over any adder we might encounter.' Most people have an aversion to snakes yet adders will retreat rather than attack whenever they can in encounters with humans. I came upon one on the hill once and when I stopped to photograph it, it slid into a hole in a clump of moss. Resisting an almost irresistible urge to grab its disappearing tail and pull it out for its portrait I, instead, raked up the moss with a handy stick and found the adder coiled up below. I secured all the photos I wanted, in no real danger despite the angry flickering of the forked tongue, and its occasional lunge forward at its tormentor. It only wanted to be left in peace, and having secured my photos I did just that.

8

Poachers, Ancient and Modern

RED deer have, all down the ages, been associated with 'privilege' right from the distant days when both fallow and red deer were royal game in the numerous forests maintained in England. Royal forests in Scotland were few in number, and in the wilder regions of the Highlands deer were probably not quite so jealously guarded, until the mid-1800s ushered in the deer-stalking era. From that time stalking became so popular as a sporting and rentable asset to estates that deer here too inevitably became associated with 'those who had' by 'those who had not'.

The fact that red deer came to be associated thus meant that, to the general public with little hope of legitimately stalking them (until the advent of stalking hotels in the 1950s), the poaching of deer became imbued with glamour. It was a tilt against authority, against the rich by the poor, a sort of Robin Hood concept in which the poacher was the hero and the owner of the land on which the deer were the villain. Because this concept died hard many otherwise right-thinking people who would have been appalled had they realized what cruelty they were protecting, turned a blind eye even in the worst days of the early 1950s when commercial poaching by road-gangs using spotlights mounted on vehicles, and shotguns to do the killing, battened on hapless deer feeding at nights wherever roads ran through the glens. 'A deer from the hill, a grouse from the heather and a fish from the river is every Highlander's right' was a popular view of the matter. Even in deer-literature poaching was as often as not written of

85

relatively sympathetically, and a book was even published called, *The Romance of Poaching in the Highlands.*

Right or wrong, the old way of poaching in which a stag or hind was taken 'for the pot' by residents in an area did relatively little harm, and many stalkers and landowners, while they obviously could not afford openly to countenance this, did yet exercise a certain amount of 'Nelson's eye'. There was undoubtedly skill and daring involved, and a tremendous amount of hard work. Legitimate stalking can be hard enough, in achieving a shot, making a clean kill and in using a pony or vehicle to get the carcase home, but the old-style poacher had also to avoid detection, ensure that his shot did not attract attention and carry his venison off the hill himself, perhaps aided by a friend. The usual way of carrying venison thus procured off the hill was to cut the carcase midway along the body, cutting through the back-bone expertly at a joint in the vertebrae and using only a knife. The half-carcase was then shouldered, with the hind or forelegs acting as 'handles', each side of the carrier's neck with the weight resting square at the back of his neck. In the case of a stag this made an extremely heavy load. I knew of three teenagers, during the last war when meat was scarce who made a foray fourteen miles into the hills and came back home all that distance carrying half a stag each in the small hours of a late summer's morning. One of them told me that his shoulders could not bear the straps of his braces next day, so 'tender' were they. This was earning their venison with a vengeance and the sheer physical graft of it, plus the risk of detection, ensured that it did not often occur.

Johnny Kytra in his forty years or so on Culachy had relatively few rubs with poachers. He was the absolute soul of probity himself and I do not think that ever in his career did he have a piece of venison or even rabbit for himself without sanction. Though he had little to say of personal encounters with poachers he had yet a fund of yarns about poaching. The one I remember best occurred in a certain West Coast forest, in a region which was notable for illicit stills, in which uisgebeath (whisky) was distilled, a practice which died hard in the remoter areas of the Highlands.

'Stalkers in the late 1800s,' said Johnny, 'were regarded as responsible if a still was found on their hill, for it was felt that they should know intimately all the ground and what was going on on it.' He spoke of the 'gaugers', or Excisemen, two of whom were billeted in Fort Augustus. 'I remember them coming into our lonely house at

86

Lagainabhainne, soaked after a long spell of spying out on the hill, and stripping naked to dry in front of our fire. They would often be out spying like this on the hill and would come into the poor shepherd's houses for shelter and food.'

The poaching incident occurred on the West Coast forest referred to when the stalker 'A' in the course of his duties stumbled on a still in full operation. He was well entertained and both parties concerned eventually went their separate ways with mutual expressions of esteem'. 'A', however, became a prey to uneasy conscience thereafter. If it was discovered that there was a still on his ground which he had not reported it could go ill with him. It seemed wiser to him to brave the certainty of the wrath of the illicit whisky-makers rather than to flout authority, and so he reported the still, and the men whose whisky he had shared.

'A' was not a West Coast man and little realized just what fierce independence he had crossed in betraying them. When the stalking season opened, and the shooting lodge was full of gentry, on its first day the head of a stag adorned each gatepost of the road to the hill. Tied to each was a label 'A present for Mr "A"'.

Explanation was asked for, and given, but the situation became unbearable as the season progressed, with, at sporadic intervals, the heads of stags, similarly labelled, turning up, and so 'A' had to go, and he left the West Coast with a deeper insight than he had arrived with.

Most poaching in the days before the 1939 war years was done for the pot or for the thrill of it. Came the war years and with a scarcity of meat venison began to be profitable, and by the early 1950s deer-poaching had entered a new and most unsavoury period in which all was subordinated to gain, and it seemed that every vestige of decency in those who battened on the deer was forgotten. The procedure was for a poaching gang to drive along at night on one of the many lonely roads in the Highlands beside which deer were known to graze in the evenings of winter and spring, and, using spotlights mounted on their vehicles, to shoot at the dazzled deer with shotguns without regard for the ones which, crippled, crept pitifully away in the darkness to die, perhaps hours, perhaps days, after the shooting. Those which dropped were bundled quickly into car or van and away the poachers went, to repeat the raid in some other unfrequented area whenever the beer money ran out.

It was during this unsavoury era, in April 1959, that I was witness

87

to the aftermath of a night-time roadside slaughter. This was at the time when the 1959 Deer Bill (Scotland) was still dragging its way through Parliament, incurring as it did so, an undue amount of unenlightened opposition. When I got home that night so disgusted, appalled and enraged was I still, that I sat down and wrote of my feelings and sent the article to *The Field*. I was later assured by a well-informed acquaintance that this, published by *The Field* on 14th May 1959, probably helped significantly in settling the issue in favour of the Bill. Be that as it may, the Bill was finally passed and, tardy as many of us thought it, it put an end to the worst of the major abuses perpetrated on red deer by the motorized poaching gangs. *The Field* article I quote from below;

'Sheer disgust has prompted me to write this, disgust evoked by the sight of some pitiful remains left lying by a roadside loch on an Inverness-shire estate a few days ago, in late April. They were shown to me by the estate stalker. We were going out to do a routine check on fox dens and he stopped the Land Rover to let me see.

'The first thing which caught my eye as I looked from the Land Rover window, at the edge of the secondary road, was the pathetic "Still-life" here reproduced—the head, legs and gralloch of a hind, and lying in the midst of these, her unborn calf, mutely appealing even in death, dappled and fully formed, as it had been torn from the mother in gralloching. It was, and is in the picture, a sight eloquent beyond words in its silent condemnation of the brutish methods employed by the poaching gangs at present [1959] operating in the Highlands. The hind was one of half a dozen, all in like condition, slaughtered, a scant few weeks before they were due to give birth to their calves, by men with no compassion in their make-up.

'These deer had come down in the evening to the sweet, new grass at the road's edge, and the usual procedure had been employed by the poachers. The deer, standing huddled and uncertain by the roadside, dazzled in the black of the night by the poacher's spotlight, had been riddled by shotguns.

'Let any decent thinking individual consider the suffering and cruelty inflicted by these callous gangsters. There have been many instances these past few months; hinds shot and their calves at foot left to starve; wounded beasts crippled and suffering, found near the roads; and, surely one of the most shocking, the reported case of the terribly wounded young stag which was bundled *alive* into a car's boot when the poachers were startled at their vile work and which

88

must have suffered unthinkable agonies of pain and fear, immured in a dark, stifling car boot, to be put out of its misery only when the car was ultimately stopped by police and stalkers.

'There has always been a certain aura of romance to the general public about deer poaching. This, as practised by a single man out for a deer for his pot, needing skill to *pick* his beast and to stalk and shoot it cleanly, with the added spice of having to avoid detection, and in a sense "earning" his beast by having the hard work of getting it home through miles of rough hill, undoubtedly has "appeal" about it.

'In the commercial, roadside poaching there is *no* romance, it is cold-blooded carnage with no danger, skill or work needed. Were it otherwise, few of these poachers would ever kill deer.'

The illustration of the pitiful remains left in full view at the quiet, peaceful roadside loch may help in fostering understanding of what this bestial type of deer-poaching entailed prior to the passing of the Deer (Scotland) Act, 1959.

On a par with the poacher of that era were the men who bought the venison, knowing full well how it was obtained and how unfit for human consumption most of it was. Outwardly respectable, did they ever, I wonder, allow themselves to think of all that this way of obtaining venison entailed, or did they simply shut eyes, ears and conscience to it? It would seem they did. If there had been no unscrupulous demand there would have been no killing in catering for this market.

To end a chapter which may bring home to my readers the fact that there is a sordid as well as a glamorous side to deer-poaching I would refer briefly to the wire-snaring of deer. *This is absolutely illegal* but it does still occur on occasion, perhaps more often in poaching roe than red deer. I have, however, experienced two instances of this barbarous, inhumane practice in killing red deer. In the first, I shot a stag early in one spring because he was raiding arable ground. Around his chest, so deeply grooved into hair, skin and flesh as to be almost invisible, was a makeshift snare of fence wire, which had broken off just above the 'slip-knot' in the snared stag's struggles. How long that stag had carried that cruelly constricting wire I hate to conjecture. Sufficient to state that it was deeply buried and grown over by a 'crusting' of flesh; one shudders to contemplate the agony that beast must have had to become inured to.

In the second instance I found a stag dead on a wooded river bank, on the fringes of arable ground. A fence-wire snare, attached to a tree, stretched taut as a fiddle string, was implacably tight around his neck and his bulging tongue spoke of his prolonged strangulation. In neither of these cases had the snarer profited by his captures; in the second case the snare was not even being attended regularly, for the stag was decomposing. I suspect that the snare here was set by someone who knew the stag was raiding arable ground and who, rather than go through the proper channels of complaint, to the estate concerned, or Red Deer Commission, had resorted to this illegal and barbarous method.

I believe, thankfully, that this inhumane and largely fruitless method of trying to kill red deer seldom occurs nowadays but when it does occur its manifest cruelty is, to say the least, such as to make one wonder about the sensibilities of those who employ it.

9

Stalking Stags and Hinds

LATE September in the Highlands can be enchanting. The short-lived vivid green of July, superseded by the imperial purples of August heather, has given place to the almost unreal orange-tawny hue of the fading deer-grass, that tint which Balfour-Browne captured superlatively in his portrayals of deer-forest life.

The lower hills are ablaze with more varied colours, with the russet of dead bracken a rich backcloth. Rowan trees are unashamedly flamboyant, often against a grey rock background, with flaming red leaves and the vermilion berries which offer rich harvest for many birds, from ring-ousel to blackcock. From these lower glens, meandering tree-fringed tendrils marking the hill-burns reach out, with here and there a brilliant splash of clear yellow, marking the spot which an isolated black poplar has found congenial to its growth. The positively clean-cut yellow of these isolated trees draws the eye like a magnet, a vivid splash in the dark background of a hill burnside and a strikingly beautiful one. How these poplars arrived on the Highland scene I do not know but individual trees occur far out in the hills, possibly bird- or wind-sown. The birch trees of the higher ground will be in shades of golden yellow while lower down many will yet be green with only clusters of gold-pieces, pendant amid the green, marking the onset of autumn.

It is against these varied backgrounds, their freshness and open-airness, their glimpses of wild life and their vistas of mountain and loch unequalled throughout Britain, that deer-stalking takes place in the Highlands, in which the surroundings far transcend the moment of the kill when a stag, so glorious in life, seems to have inexplicably shrunk to mediocrity in death, a part of the wild hills gone for ever.

The fact is undeniable, however, that deer-stalking must always be part of the Highland scene, as a *necessary* method of control, in the lack of any major natural predators on adult red deer. Such control as Nature does exert nowadays is simply a weeding out in the lean time of March and April, of the unfit, mainly weak youngsters or aged adults. Very few deer die naturally in the Highlands between the ages of two and, say, ten years old. If deer were left uncropped by the rifle, population would build up to such an extent eventually that they would destroy their own habitat progressively in overgrazing. They would also overspill onto adjacent marginal arable ground and into woodlands to a very much greater extent than today.

Deer-stalking is in many ways the direct antithesis of the ways of modern life, in which the trend is increasingly to cosset humanity from physical exertion and to insulate it from the realities of cold and wet, in overheated cars and habitations. Even nowadays, with mechanization creeping into the hills also, with Land Rovers and tracked vehicles replacing the use of ponies and of human legs, there still remains much physical effort, for vehicles can go only so far on the hills and will, I sincerely hope, be regarded by the stalker only as transport *to* and *from* the hill, and not abused as a means of approaching so near to the quarry as to make a mockery of stalking, and to rob it of all achievement.

True deer-stalking necessitates keen eyes and the ability to walk long distances (not necessarily at a fast pace, though there are undeniably times when fleetness of foot is a great asset), and to tackle patiently long, circuitous approaches; to crawl on hands and knees for lengthy periods over extremes of terrain from the relative comfort of dry, mossy ridges to the extreme discomfort of icy burn or mucky peat bogs; to wriggle forward belly flat, also under these varying conditions, flat indeed as the proverbial flounder, keeping pressed to the surface even when sharp rock or chilly wetness seems to penetrate to the very vitals. Above all it needs *patience* in walking to find one's deer, in spying them to *select* a suitable beast, in the final painstaking approach and, perhaps most difficult of all for most sportsmen, in the last wait at the firing point until the painfully won situation is just right for the climax of the shot. The least lapse of patience at this point, in fidgeting or hasty movement, while 'under the eyes' of deer, can lead to the complete nullification of lengthy hours of preparation, selection and approach work. At the best, one may then have to be satisfied with a hasty stalk in the shortness of time left, on another beast on which less careful selection can be spared, at the worst, a fruitless day.

In all his forty years of stalking Johnny Kytra had never seen a Land Rover employed in stalking on Culachy, though in his latter days he used to ride to the hill, over a rough 'road' in a small cart pulled by the deer-pony. He had seen many tenants, for Culachy had been let annually as a rule and of most of them he had some yarn or other.

He had once watched a stag canter off at the rear of his hinds apparently untouched by the shot. A slightly smaller stag, which had been lying at a discreet distance above this herd, suddenly rose as they passed below and, charging down at the stag with the hinds, bowled him over, stabbing at him with his antlers, before running off after the hinds and leaving the prostrate stag behind. Wondering greatly, the stalking party went up to find that the fallen stag had succumbed to the shot and not to the furious onslaught of the attacking stag, for he had quite literally been dying on his feet when the second stag, probably one bested by him previously when in full possession of his strength, had sensed his weakness and, characteristically, had taken immediate advantage of it.

Johnny had had an experience with an apparently pugnacious stag one season which 'gave me quite a start'. He had been alone, bending down, gralloching a stag he'd just shot, when some instinct made him swing around to look behind him. There, almost breathing down his neck, was a huge, black-maned, wide-antlered stag, fixedly regarding him. Johnny believed that the combined odours of blood and rutting 'aroma' of the dead stag had drawn in the 'travelling' stag, while serving to disguise his own human scent.

He had had one or two instances of following up wounded stags as most stalkers have had and in one case darkness had defeated them though they knew the stag must be lying down near at hand. Johnny had apparently not had much of a look at the head of the stag except at long range through his stalking-glass. Next morning they set off early for the whereabouts of the wounded stag and picked him up almost at once. Wriggling in, the *coup de grâce* was administered.

'I couldn't make out the shape of his head at all as we wriggled

in,' said Johnny, 'there was something queer about it.' Queer
indeed, for it proved to be a three-antlered stag.

My own unforgettable experience in following up a wounded stag
entailed a day-long pursuit and a chapter of misadventure. This stag,
a one-antlered one, had swung away *just* as the shot was fired and
had consequently been wounded instead of cleanly killed, at 10.30
a.m., on an October day when the hill, fortunately, as it transpired,
had been covered by an overnight fall of snow. I took the rifle from
the tenant with only the remaining rounds in the magazine and
followed the stag, which was going away steadily, though obviously
hit. An attempt to shoot him at long range before he went out onto a
huge flat, where I knew I would have to wait until he got out of sight
before I could pursue unseen, failed, mainly because I was using a
'strange' rifle and allowed too much elevation for the range. The stag
was now left behind by his erstwhile harem, but although he slowed
down temporarily he kept getting spurred on by the alarm of the
many deer which were in that area on that day, and which I had
unavoidably to disturb in attempting to keep in touch with the
wounded beast. Twice, I *had* to lose sight of him but each time
picked him up again from a commanding ridge, each time however
with a widening gap between us.

He then joined up with five other stags and they all settled about
five miles from where he had been shot, on a very open face. Owing
to this and the snow-covered ground I had great difficulty in getting
within range, and when I did press trigger on him only a noisy
'click' came—a misfire—and at that moment of all times. Away he
went again, alone once more, and a hurried shot as he went once
more was too high. I had now to wait until he got over a distant skyline so that he would not see me and then, on protesting legs, tracked
him up the hill-face in the snow.

We were well out on the snow-covered high ground now and there
was not another deer, or, fortunately, track to be seen. I did not
actually see my quarry again, so far ahead had he got, until I finally
caught up with him. He had first gone straight uphill while I had
waited below, but, out of my sight, had turned off abruptly at right
angles among the high-ground peat hags. Without the evidence of his
tracks in the snow I must have lost him then, for I would have carried
straight on in the hope of finding him in a big, sheltered coire which
I knew lay ahead. A little way farther on his tracks betrayed his
apparently evasive tactics again: he had gone *into* a burn, as if to go

94

uphill along its course but had turned, in the burn, where no tracks betrayed him, and gone *downhill*. This I discovered after I worked up the bed of the burn until a waterfall barred further progress. Yet there were no tracks to mark where the stag had climbed out and so I turned back downstream and found out how he had fooled me. After emerging well down the burn he had again turned off at right angles, among broken peat hags, and made as if to go straight down into the Spey valley, now about ten miles from where the pursuit had begun.

I cut straight down here, only to find I had been too clever, and had overshot his tracks. He had *again* doubled back, and waded up a smaller burn for some distance before going off at right angles once more. A very little farther on and I almost fell over him, my first inkling that I had caught up being the fortunate sight of an antler-tip sticking up above the small hillock behind which he now lay. I had followed these last five miles with only one bullet left, the one which had previously misfired, in the hope (as often occurs) that it would fire when tried again. Unsure of whether this, my only bullet, would fire or not, I lay doubting, watching the unsuspecting stag, until my position on the exposed, snow-covered, high ground became unendurable. Was he near death? Could I rush him and administer the *coup de grâce* with my knife? If the rifle misfired could he rise again for another marathon upon hearing the 'click'? It became obvious that unless I tried something I would be too frozen to shoot accurately, and so I took a careful and prayerful sight on his neck. To my boundless relief the bullet fired and so ended the marathon pursuit, some six hours and ten roundabout miles from where I'd started. Had it not been for the snow I had inevitably lost him in his evasive tactics. Whether these tactics were premeditated or fortuitous, I can only conjecture but certainly, if it had been a 'thinking' human who had employed them one would have had no hesitation in believing them as 'of design'.

A more pleasant 'long day' I once spent with the 'rifle' I had out, right on the summit of our highest top, lying beside its cairn, from 2 p.m. on a sunny afternoon until 7 p.m. in the evening. It was early in the season and while we had the enjoyment of watching a big herd of hinds below us, on our ground, there was no stag with them. However, about a mile away, over the march, there lay three stags, roaring lazily at intervals throughout that long afternoon. Naboth's vineyard indeed, but we had no other prospect in view and so we lay waiting and enjoying our sweeping vista of mountains and deer. I was certain that with the wind blowing *out* of our ground the stags would come *into* it, to our hinds in the evening and so it transpired. About 6 p.m. the three stags began grazing and slowly approaching the march, while we watched tensely and wondered if stags or darkness would arrive first. In the event we had to make a very quick but cautious and intensely thrilling stalk to cut off our stag, for the one we selected quickened pace considerably as he came in. It was still broad daylight when we got him but my signals, from the skyline, to the pony-man went unnoticed. He had had a very long wait and had obviously become careless. This delayed us considerably for I had a very long drag with the stag, from 3,000 feet to river level, while I sent the 'rifle' back to the jeep which we had left, miles away in a different direction, on Wade's road. It was 9.30 p.m. and pitch dark before I got to the pony-man and he thought we were going home then. In this I had to disillusion him. The stag lay a mile away and by the time we went back for him, loaded him and eventually got home, all in the dark, it was near midnight. We arrived just in time to meet a search party setting out to look for us.

Regarding the jeep already referred to, this was a remarkable, and at times, provoking vehicle which on occasion bade fair to end my stalking career, more so than any other hazard on the hill. It was on loan to us at the stag-stalking season so that 'rifles', of widely-varying fitness, would not have to walk too far. It was also undeniably useful in relieving the pony of the stag once he got it to Wade's road. This vehicle, which I came to regard with affectionate horror, had no self-starter, hardly any brakes and an unpredictable quirk of stopping dead in the middle of swollen hill-burns. From one such burn which crossed our road, I remember we had to manhandle it back up the slope out of the raging burn, up to our thighs in its icy waters. Luckily there were four of us that day or we had never succeeded. On another occasion, also a very wet day, a happy-go-lucky character who made even that drab day enjoyable, went back for the jeep while I contacted the pony-man to take the stag to where the jeep could collect it. The jeep was across a burn, now swollen in spate, and the starting handle was needed to start her, my 'rifle' jumping in hastily as she reluctantly 'fired', and charging through the ford in a bow-wave of yellow-brown water. A little way farther on the jeep cut-out. The driver sprang out and rummaged for the starting handle. Then he suddenly realized, appalled, that he had left it stuck in the engine when he had hurriedly leapt in to take the

96

The red deer stag, magnificent in life.

Pitifully, magnificence shrunk to mediocrity. An illegally snared stag, mouth open as it choked horribly and agonizingly to death.

XLII

Head, legs and gralloch of a hind shot by road-gang poachers, in its midst the dappled form of her unborn calf.

XLIII · A travelling stag at the time of the rut, thrusting impatiently through the hill, abandoning the unattainable for the illusory.

A fine stag with his harem of hinds on a typically misty October day in the Monadliaths.

A stag holding hinds on the high tops in the early part of the rutting season, watchful and suspicious, ever alert for possible rivals.

XLIV

Roaring, a challenge and a warning, while the hinds placidly chew their cuds in pointed contrast to the fever of their overlord.

To me, there is no sound so evocative of the Highlands in October as the roaring of the red deer stags.

XLV

Spying for hinds in the whiteness of the winter hills.

XLVI

Hinds in winter, in a pattern of white snow and leafless birches.

XLVII

In a driving blizzard of snow Prince, the pony, became transformed from black to a dirty grey.

After a day's hind stalking in deep snow the welcome prospect of nearing home.

XLVIII

jeep on. It was no longer there, needless to say, and he found it lying, luckily in the shallows, in the burn he had charged through. It was bent into a shape which no starting handle was ever meant to assume and we had to take it to a semi-ruinous stone bothy nearby and partially straighten it in the interstices of the stone wall before we could get it into sufficient resemblance to a starting handle to get our jeep started.

Coming in off the hill that day, this 'rifle', a rather beefy young man, was so filthy with crawling in peat that he decided he must really wash his black feet before climbing into the bath in the hotel where he was staying. Alas for his thoughtfulness. In plonking one great black foot into the rather (it would seem) fragile washbasin he put it right through it. A man of some resource he immediately summoned a fellow-rifle or two, also staying in this stalking-hotel and they pieced the desecrated washbasin together, 'but when some idiot ran the hot tap it fell to pieces again'. I believe he was a distinctly unpopular guest with the management, if not with his fellow guests, on that occasion.

More than once we watched deer scatter as an eagle, or eagles, glided low above them and indeed, if geese or whooper swans on autumnal migration flew unduly low over the heads of deer they also temporarily scattered the herd, so that it appeared that the near approach of any large bird was a matter for dread to the deer, an association from calfhood perhaps. A reliable friend, stalker on a neighbouring estate, had two others with him when in the early October of 1968 they witnessed an eagle attack a small herd of half a dozen deer, which ran in panic-stricken flight. Twice they watched the eagle single out and land on the head and neck of a four-month-old calf, flapping and balancing with huge wings, clutching with steel-clawed talons and, he said, pecking at the head as it rode its panic-stricken steed. The chase went out of sight before they witnessed its result but I suspect the end was inevitable.

Not content with the season's stalking, when one had often to subordinate the enjoyment of watching deer to the realities of the stalk, it was my habit to frequent the hill after the stalking, taking note of the activity and of the stags left, for future reference.

From my notes of 1966: 'To those interested in deer there can be no sound as evocative of the Highlands in October as the roaring of the rutting stags, which fills the normally silent glens then, thrilling, yet in some measure, daunting also. Thus I reflected as I lay, late one

October afternoon, high up on the rocky face of a long, narrow glen, and listened with real pleasure to the very voice of the darkening hills. I should have been on my way home long since for I had a two-hour walk before I would reach it, yet I lay on, savouring the noise and spectacle as deer drew in slowly along the glen, for their evening grazing, each lot of hinds with its attendant vociferous overlord of the moment, while above, or below, or behind, sundry as yet unsuccessful aspirants to marital privileges lurked, or impatiently thrust on through the hills, abandoning the unattainable for the illusory. Most of these "travellers" were black with peat wallowing, impregnated with the rank rutting odour and loud-voiced in their desires.'

While the rut ended for the big stags about the end of October, the younger staggies carried it on well into November, and indeed I have heard sporadic roaring in December and even in January. This being so, even although I did not believe in beginning to stalk hinds until mid November, although the *legal* season allows it from 21st October there was usually still an overlap of some slight rutting activity when I started. This led to a rather humorous episode in November 1965, as I noted: 'As usual there was still some roaring to be heard as a few young staggies strove to emulate, without real success, the swash-buckling of their elders, who had long since lost all interest in the few hinds still in season. Owing to this, a rather comical situation arose on our very first day out, when three brothers, stalking enthusiasts from England, were out with me. Comical at least to the two who, some way behind us with the pony, were able to watch it unfold.

'I and the chap who was to take the shot had got to within one hundred and fifty yards of a small herd of hinds, with which there was a young stag who was bellowing, rather than roaring, at intervals. The deer were lying, most uncharacteristically, in deep, frosty shade in the lee of a ridge, while we lay behind a knoll which was in full sun, clear of the cold shadow cast by the high ridge ahead. For some time we had had to lie there waiting for the sun to shift round a bit; its rays were shining directly into the telescopic sight of the rifle, making it unwise to try a shot. I felt certain that the deer would not remain long in such chill shade as they lay in and, sure enough, at intervals they began to rise and drift, sun-seeking, along the face from us, picking mouthfuls as they leisurely went. A few remained, however, including the staggie, and so we also remained. Watching, we saw the stag rise next and begin to wander across in our direction, and at first we thought little of this. He walked and grazed steadily nearer, however, and was at last on the very top of the knoll below which we crouched, petrified, hardly daring to breathe, enjoying (though that scarcely describes our feelings then) the sight of a stag at *fifteen yards'* range.

'Now in full, warming sunlight the staggie decided to lie down, while I struggled between amusement and exasperation. I had had the opposite sex spoil both stalks on stag and hind respectively but seldom in such a blatant manner. We were absolutely pinned down, unable to move a muscle, far less to poke the rifle muzzle over the shielding knoll to try for a hind. I could readily visualize the suppressed mirth of our audience of two, enjoying the sight of stalkers "stalked"—my own reaction had I been in their place.

'At last, of course, the inevitable happened when a stag is lying within fifteen yards, looking straight towards one's place of scant concealment. He spotted a slight movement and, getting up, walked, stilted-legged with suspicion, around our recumbent forms. His nose told him, as he circled into the wind, what his eyes had failed to discriminate, and he forthwith stampeded back to the hinds, taking them away in his alarm. We got two hinds later that day and could then enjoy the humour of a situation scarcely appreciated at the time.'

Of conditions of heavy snow I wrote in January 1962: 'With the heavy overnight fall the mundane, tree-lined path to the hill had been miraculously transformed. The unique fairyland quality of the scene held much to appreciate in its beauty, the thinnest of twigs on every tree balancing its tier of snow with all the aplomb of a professional juggler. Even the very slightest breath of wind would dispel some of the enchantment but, meantime, it was there to enjoy. The tangible silence of land under deep snow was periodically rent by a loud creaking "crack", as here and there a protesting branch gave up the struggle to sustain its burden. Fairyland or no, the going, with the pony following, was arduous, every step lifted high to clear the deep, soft snow, leg muscles complaining at each step. In the deep snow the pony could walk faster than I and every so often a hoof would crack me on the back of a leg, his nose simultaneously prodding at my back as if to ask why I was so unusually slow. Some of the cross-gullies which we had to negotiate were drifted waist-high. No question of lifting one's legs high enough to clear them, one had to use one's body as a battering-ram, forcing a way through.'

One was very conscious, each winter, of the almost incredible hardihood of Highland wildlife, not just occasional hardihood needed on rare occasions in a lifetime, but a patient endurance necessary *every* long winter, on the hills, in order simply to survive. I have seen grouse fly slowly ahead of me with tail feathers stiff in a white encasement of frosted snow. I have found a mallard duck frozen into the ice of a pond and I have seen, often, red deer hinds with back and neck hairs a stiff bristle of frost. And yet they survive, and thrive, in those conditions annually.

Despite the inclemency of the weather which each hind-stalking season afforded in good measure, my two sons, Lea and Michael, were ever anxious to accompany me whenever chance offered. They had done so from a very early age, going out on the deer saddle of the pony, in snow, before they were five years old. As they grew older their aid became an asset to add to the pleasure of their youthful zest. One cannot, however, go a lot to the winter-hills and always avoid unpleasant situations, and one such episode nearly, very nearly, ended in tragedy. From my notes of December 1966: 'I had promised Lea and Michael, 15 and 12 respectively, that I would take them hind-stalking while they had their Christmas holidays. On a day in late December, then, we left early for the hill, the boys leading two ponies. There had been heavy rain nearly all the previous night and it was still showery as we left home in the half-light. The hill-burns were roaring in a spate of melting snow waters each adding its yeasty quota to the already bank-high waters of the river our path followed, a turgid, yellow-brown torrent in which no rocks were visible. I had taken my two rifles so that I could "cover up" with one while a boy used the other.

'The milder, though wet, conditions had taken the deer high and we took the ponies about seven miles before we left them tied securely on a long rein to a tree, and munching contentedly enough on the hay carried out on the deer saddles.

'We had to cross one of the larger hill-burns and managed this only with the aid of a fallen tree, which almost spanned it. A party of hinds was working across the face ahead, high up, coming in towards the upper reaches of the burn we had crossed. By the time we had climbed the steep face some of them had actually crossed the burn and were in a favourable place for stalking. Because of this we had to re-cross the burn, but to do so we had now to cross at a place where the burn gouged its turbulent way between constricting, rocky sides.

100

Below our crossing point the burn dropped all of two hundred feet in a succession of foaming waterfalls, culminating in a sheer, rocky fall of fifty feet before racing to join the main river. At the crossing place I chose we were just on the lip of one of those falls, but a convenient large rock in midstream offered a reasonable stepping stone, though the current was rushing, deceptively smooth, over its rounded top.

'I put an exploratory foot on the rock and the icy snow-water mounted at once up my leg and gushed around it, filling my long rubber boot. The tug of that current was quite obviously going to be too much for the boys, unaided, and so I took the two rifles on my back so as to leave them unhampered. I then stepped out again, and this time, so narrow was the confined channel, stood with one foot on the rock and one on the other side of the burn in order to steady the boys as they crossed. Ready thus, I told Michael to cross first, and in a trice he was over at the expense of water-filled boots. Lea came forward then and so quickly that I still have no clear recollection of how it happened, he was in the maelstrom of raging water and being swept towards the falls. I made a desperate lunge forward, caught him somehow and somewhere, but off balance I could not hold him against the pull of the eager current. There was, of course, no question of letting go and with a sousing splash in I went after him, an unreasoning action which simply said, "Get the boy out", with neither time nor desire to consider anything else. The force of the water on the brink of the falls was quite irresistible and over we went, hurly burly in a tangle of arms, legs and rifles to land with sodden impact in the pool below and go deep under. Only then did I form the conscious thought, "We've had it now", for to go out of one's depth in a burn swollen with melting snow, with two rifles heavy on one's back, while struggling to maintain a hold on a lad shocked with the suddenness of it all, and with the awareness of the big falls below, was no experience calculated to make one hopeful of survival. Hardly had I formulated the thought than a kick of my feet brought us to the surface and, simultaneously, a swirl of the current swept us momentarily towards one side of the rocky bowl we were in. I suddenly felt bottom below my feet and, up to my neck in the pool, managed to shove Lea ahead of me, gasping, poor lad, with shock, towards the bank. There Michael was already crouched, having raced down the burn-side after us, to grip the collar of his anorak and while I shoved he pulled and up the rock-face went Lea, burn water cascading from him. I clambered slowly after him, shuddering a little

Index

Index

Roman numerals refer to plates

105

107